Fifty years of Brittany Ferries

MILES COWSILL · RICHARD KIRKMAN

Published by:
Ferry Publications, Registered Office, Ballachrink Beg, Jurby East, Ramsey, Isle of Man IM7 3HD
Tel: +44 (0) 1624 898446
E-mail: info@lilypublications.co.uk Website: www.ferrypubs.co.uk

ISBN: 9781911268673

Produced and designed by Lily Publications Ltd.
Printed and bound in Wales.

Published by Lily Publications Ltd on behalf of Ferry Publications.
Registered office: Ballachrink Beg, Jurby East, Ramsey, Isle of Man, IM7 3HD.
Tel: +44 (0)1624 898446
Email: ferrypubs@manx.net
Web: www.ferrypubs.co.uk

A CIP catalogue record for this book is available from the British Library.

Contents

Introduction

The authors began their relationships with Brittany Ferries from two different perspectives, illustrating the strengths of the Company's foundations.

As proprietor of the leading Ferry Publications publishing house, and publisher of the authoritative quarterly magazine *Ferry & Cruise Review*, Miles Cowsill has enjoyed a long-standing relationship with Brittany Ferries. He first encountered the Company when reporting news and developments for the magazine as Brittany Ferries expanded rapidly in the 1980s, and worked closely with the marketing and on board teams to plan a number of specialist Enthusiasts' weekends to experience the growing route structure.

From the outset Brittany Ferries was highly and enthusiastically supportive of relationships with those who had an interest the Company, its ships, and its history, seeking to cultivate the support of those who became some if its strongest advocates. Many individuals went out of their way to support the enthusiast community and provide timely news information.

The desire to ensure that the story of Brittany Ferries was well recorded and that milestones were celebrated with appropriate record extended to the publication of a series of books to commemorate successive decades of operation. This enthusiasm extended to recording the arrival of new vessels in book form, providing a permanent archive of the evolution of the design and style for which the Company became synonymous.

Ian Carruthers and David Longden, in particular, were immensely supportive in recognising the value of cultivating relationships and the importance of the written record. Their leadership set the tone for the Company, and Ferry Publications has long enjoyed the support, friendship, and commitment from a wide range of staff at sea and on shore, from Senior Masters to the marketing team. The half-century of progress which this books portrays is fitting testament to their collective efforts.

Richard Kirkman found himself working in competition with Brittany Ferries' joint-venture Channel Islands Ferries operation when the company inaugurated services in 1985, in his role as Freight Manager for Sealink British Ferries' routes from Portsmouth and Weymouth. When the two operations merged as British Channel Island Ferries he was one of the few to transfer from Sealink to the company, taking up the role of Sales Manager for the new enterprise. Later he joined P&O European Ferries'

The *Pont-Aven* arrives at Plymouth to undertake berthing trials for the first time. *(Miles Cowsill)*

Bretagne *(Pascal Bredel)*

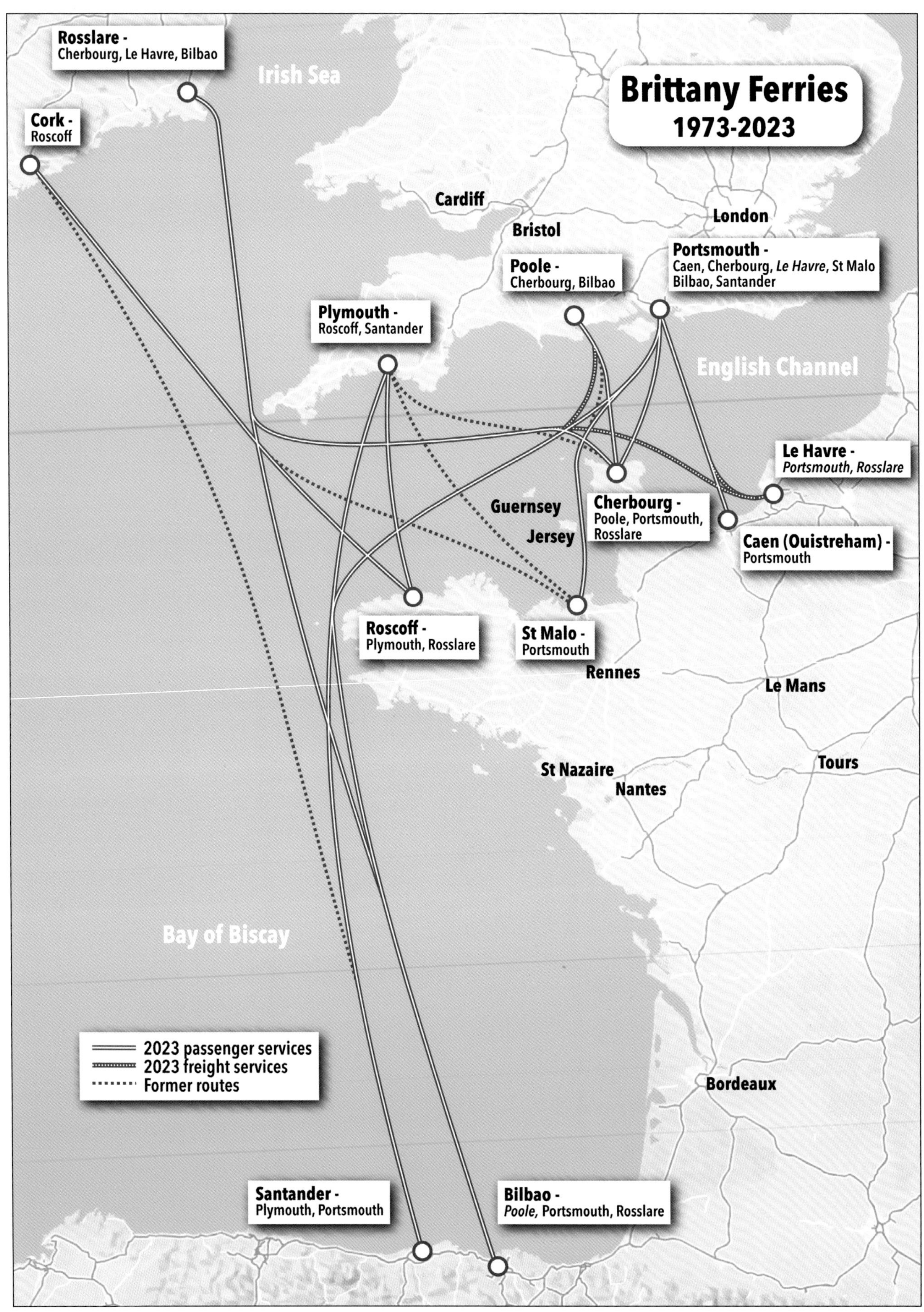
Brittany Ferries
1973-2023
Rosslare -
Cherbourg, Le Havre, Bilbao
Irish Sea
Cork -
Roscoff
Cardiff
Bristol
London
Poole -
Cherbourg, Bilbao
Portsmouth -
Caen, Cherbourg, *Le Havre*, St Malo
Bilbao, Santander
Plymouth -
Roscoff, Santander
English Channel
Le Havre -
Portsmouth, Rosslare
Guernsey
Jersey
Cherbourg -
Poole, Portsmouth,
Rosslare
Caen (Ouistreham) -
Portsmouth
Roscoff -
Plymouth, Rosslare
St Malo -
Portsmouth
Rennes
Le Mans
St Nazaire
Nantes
Tours
Bay of Biscay
2023 passenger services
2023 freight services
Former routes
Bordeaux
Santander -
Plymouth, Portsmouth
Bilbao -
Poole, Portsmouth, Rosslare

Portsmouth services as Head of Passenger Marketing & Sales and found himself again competing directly with Brittany Ferries.

The two companies employed very different strategies as they sought to gain market share on the Western Channel. Yet they shared a common foe as they each sought to counter the challenge of the Channel Tunnel and the damaging price war precipitated on the short sea cross-Channel routes.

Brittany Ferries was embarking on the sustained long term investment programme that provided the foundations for the Company's future success, whilst P&O European Ferries' Board was content to take a shorter-term view and charter the 'Olau' twins and the *Pride of Bilbao* at crippling expense for the local operation. Attempts to bring the two companies together came to naught and it is a matter of history that Brittany Ferries is the sole survivor today.

Relationships between the two companies remained respectful and cordial throughout the competitive era, and passengers benefitted from the mutual drive to improve customer service. Brittany Ferries brought an increasingly uncanny knack to 'predict and provide' the right services on the right routes as the Company expanded. The high calibre management team brought a strong emphasis on quality with a market-focussed approach, embodied in the branding concept of the French (and Spanish) holiday beginning the moment the vessel was boarded. Coupled with an in-house market leading inclusive holiday product, the gallic flair delivered by the catering and accommodation teams, and strong supportive relationships with the French regions, this all made Brittany Ferries a formidable competitor.

The later opportunity to work with successive directors of Brittany Ferries' UK operation to compile the book *'Brittany Ferries – from a cause to a brand'* provided an valuable insight into just how this impressive success had been achieved, whilst increasing the admiration of the drive, passion, commitment and focus of those responsible for delivering it.

As Brittany Ferries celebrated 50 years of operation the Company can look back at a track record of success, despite the often-turbulent trading conditions that have characterised the first half-century. The original enduring principles have served the operation well, and the founders would recognise the continuation of the long-term perspective and the strong symbiotic relationship with local communities that characterised the operation back in 1973.The Company has overcome a succession of challenges that would have long sunk a less committed operator and fully deserves the dominant market position that it now enjoys. The next half-century can be faced with confidence.

Miles Cowsill
Isle of Man

Richard Kirkman
East Sussex
December 2022

The *Cap Finistère* was to prove one of the most successful second-hand purchases in the company's fifty years of operations. The German-built ship, one of a series of twelve near-sisters, is seen seen here leaving Le Havre during her last season on the English Channel. *(Pascal Bredel)*

Salamanca **and *Mont St Michel* at Portsmouth.** *(Mike Louagie)*

Origins

Brittany in the 1960s was an isolated region of France, experiencing the disadvantages of geographical and political isolation from the Parisian government. Local farmers had no direct ferry link to lucrative export markets across the English Channel after British Railways closed their Southampton-St Malo service at the end of the 1964 summer season; London lay closer to the region than did Paris. Thoresen Car Ferries stepped into the breach at Southampton, but from a Breton perspective their new services operated to the distant ports of Cherbourg and Le Havre. Export produce faced a long overland journey from Brittany and was often displaced at the port by fresher Normandy products prioritised by local Norman dockers.

Breton farmers' leader Alexis Gourvennec led discussions with the government to secure a programme of investment to support the region's development. This culminated in the announcement of the 'Sixth State Plan' in October 1968, which included investment in a deep-water port at Roscoff, a town with a long history of shipping links to England. As work began on the new facilities, Gourvennec's attention turned to attracting an operator. Although Britain was due to join the EEC in 1973 and local support for a service was strong, the route's potential was not recognised by any of the established operators. Frustratingly, they collectively turned down Gourvennec's approaches, and he faced the political and economic embarrassment of having secured funding for new port facilities that had no customers.

The farmers were already a well organised group and had established the 'Prince de Bretagne' vegetable brand in 1970; Gourvennec was president of the Société d'Intérêt Collectif Agricole (SICA) of Saint-Pol-de-Léon, a producer-led marketing organisation. As works at Roscoff neared completion, André Colin, president of the general council of Finistère, brought together a group of regional leaders, including Gourvennec, on 18th April 1972 to solve the ferry problem. Jean Hénaff, a former naval captain with shipping experience, was invited to help break the deadlock; if others weren't interested, then the Bretons would establish their own shipping line. Hénaff, Gourvennec on behalf of the SICA, and Jean Guyomarc'h, president of the Morlaix Chamber of Commerce, each pledged FF5,000 to create a public limited company with FF15,000 capital, for this purpose. The ambitious name 'Bretagne Angleterre Irlande S.A.' (BAI) was chosen for the new enterprise and the

The *Kerisnel* heads out to sea from Roscoff. *(Ferry Publications Library)*

Early construction work at the port at Roscoff. *(Ferry Publications Library)*

Company was quickly registered at the Commercial Court of Brest on 29th April 1972, with Hénaff as president.

A team was brought together in the new BAI office in rue Saint-Mathieu in Quimper to establish the Company in the freight market, acquire year-round traffic to sustain the business and, later, to develop a tourist business. The most pressing need was to find a ro-ro vessel to operate the service. Hénaff found the *Lilac*, at the Astilleros & Construcciones S.A. yard in Vigo, Spain. Launched on 22nd April 1971, she was built as a tank carrier with a heavily reinforced deck plate but was no longer required by her Israeli owners. At 99.17 metres in length, 3,395-gt and with a service speed of 18 knots, she was very suitable for the proposed BAI service, and could carry twelve passengers and 540 lane-metres of freight traffic, equivalent to 45 commercial vehicles, but came at the higher than anticipated price of FF18 million. Banks were generally reluctant to commit to an untried company for this sum, so Gourvennec persuaded his colleagues to raise the capital of BAI to FF4.5 million and secured a loan from the Crédit Agricole bank to borrow the remainder. One of BAI's first acts was to rename the vessel *Kerisnel*, after the produce auction market of the SICA Saint-Pol-de-Léon.

A number of English ports were considered as destinations for the new ferry service; Poole and Weymouth offered a comparatively short drive to the main produce markets in the Southeast and Midlands, but a longer sea crossing from Roscoff. Plymouth offered a shorter sea crossing, enabling a round trip to be encompassed each day, but lay further away from these markets. However, the UK motorway network was

Alexis Gourvennec on his farm at Morlaix. *(Brittany Ferries)*

The ship that started it all. The *Kerisnel* in her simple early livery, with the initials BAI proudly displayed on her twin funnels. *(Ferry Publications Library)*

gradually extending south westwards, and BAI opted for the shorter sea crossing to Plymouth. The British Transport Docks Board awarded a contract for the necessary work at Millbay Docks, including installation of a 180-foot linkspan, the development of a two-acre area of land for marshalling, and dredging. Meanwhile, the freight traffic phase of the Roscoff port work was completed in September 1972 at a final cost of FF17 million.

Several Breton staff moved to Plymouth to prepare for the new operation, but BAI turned to an established partner to help market the new service in the UK. The SICA Saint-Pol-de-Léon energetically promoted their vegetable products under the 'Prince de Bretagne' banner; advertising agency Bryan, Constantinidi & Brightwell (BCB) already undertook this work in the UK and embraced the challenge of marketing the new ferry. Partner Derek Brightwell proposed a corporate rebranding of BAI for the British audience, suggesting 'Brittany Ferries', for its strong geographical associations and ease of understanding. The Board agreed and henceforth 'Brittany Ferries' became the Company brand, although BAI remained the name of the Holding Company. Advertising in the UK bore the new brand from the outset.

The *Kerisnel* provided the Company's first income with a one-month charter on P&O Normandy Ferries' Southampton-Le Havre route from 13th November 1972, under the command of the Breton captain Ernest Lainé and chief officer Gérard Le Saux, who, like many of the crew, were former employees of P&O Normandy Ferries. A large crowd assembled for the arrival of the *Kerisnel* returned to Roscoff on 18th December 1972a freshly painted vessel with an all-white hull split by a single thin horizontal blue band and the initials BAI proudly displayed on her twin funnels and she was christened the *Kerisnel* by Annie Gourvennec.

More than 3,000 people gathered on the pier on the evening of 2nd January 1973 to witness the loading of *Kerisnel's* maiden commercial departure to Plymouth. The first freight customer was 28-year-old Jean Claude Rolland with a cargo of apples, bound for the Cornwall Wholesale market in Redruth. The ship's load comprised of four lorries loaded with cauliflowers, three with apples, one with lettuce, one carrying paper for Senior Service cigarettes, three empty vehicles and one car, a green Citroën Ami 6. The *Kerisnel* left on time at 23:00 with her crew supplemented by 13 passengers, arriving at Millbay Docks at 07:00 the following morning, and returning at 11:00 with four empty trailers, one loaded lorry and just one accompanying driver.

Three sailings were programmed in each direction every week, but during the height of the produce season these increased to five a week. Brittany Ferries carried 17,000 tons of traffic during the first three months, well below the 40,000 tons planned; the Company found it needed to demonstrate its resilience before hauliers would commit to the service.

The Board was keen to test demand for a passenger service from the 1974 season, and these plans were made public in March 1973. Confidence was such that an order for a multi-purpose vessel capable of carrying 80 passengers and 40 freight vehicles was placed with the Société Nouvelle des Ateliers & Chantiers of La Rochelle-Pallice, with the ship to be named *Penn-Ar-Bed* after the Breton translation of Finistère, or 'Land's End' in English.

The launch of the *Penn-Ar-Bed* on 17th May 1973 at the Société Nouvelle des Ateliers & Chantiers shipyard at La Rochelle-Pallice. *(Ferry Publications Library)*

The *Poseidon* operated for Vedettes Armoricaines to provide the first passenger service between Roscoff and Plymouth. *(Ferry Publications Library)*

Early experience and testing of the passenger market came from a short-term relationship with the Brest shipping company Vedettes Armoricaines, whose fleet included the chartered 1,363-gt *Poseidon*. The 1,358-gt, 66.5-metre-long 805-passenger capacity *Poseidon* was built by Ulstein M/V A/S in Norway in 1964 to a Knud E. Hansen design, as the second vessel operated by the emerging Stena Line. She was designed as a daytime sailing vessel. The *Poseidon* ran in parallel with the *Kerisnel* from 15th May to 15th September 1973, operating to the Trinity Pier in Millbay Docks. At first the service was rather erratic, and on some occasions the

The *Penn-Ar-Bed* and *Prince de Bretagne* pictured at Roscoff together in April 1975. *(Ferry Publications Library)*

ship did not sail to England due to a lack of custom, but by the end of the season she was averaging 120 passengers per sailing; there was clearly demand.

There was an increase in freight capacity and competition on the western Channel routes from June 1973 when the *Antelope* began operating from Poole to Cherbourg for a new company called Truckline. This freight-only service was supported by Poole Harbour Commissioners, who invested in land reclamation and built a terminal with a 22-metre linkspan and a side-loading ramp to attract the car export business. The *Antelope* was joined later in the year by the *Dauphin de Cherbourg*, but the two vessels quickly proved inadequate for the service as the growth of the company was encouragingly rapid.

The new *Penn-Ar-Bed* was launched on 17th May 1973, with her passenger complement gradually upped during construction to 150, then 320 at the end of the *Poseidon's* operating season. Her completion was delayed by shipyard strikes during the autumn, but growing optimism was justified by advance public interest in the passenger service. However, the cost of the *Penn-Ar-Bed*

The bar on the *Penn-Ar-Bed*. *(Ferry Publications Library)*

The first crew of the *Kerisnel*, Francis Jan, Chief Engineer, Commandant Ernest Lainé and Gérard Le Saux, Second Captain. *(Ferry Publications Library)*

rose to FF30 million, requiring an increase in capital, largely sourced from the SICA Saint-Pol-de-Léon and further bank borrowings. A loss of FF7 million against revenues of FF7 million in the first year forced shareholders to dig deep, but Brittany Ferries had transported 5,932 freight vehicles, with numbers growing steadily and generating optimism. However, plans to convert the *Kerisnel* to provide a second passenger operation were placed on hold, and she became surplus to requirements.

The *Penn-Ar-Bed* undertook sea trials in mid-January 1974, followed quickly be her maiden departure for Plymouth on 24th January. The timing was inauspicious, at the height of a four-fold rise in oil prices, and a sequence of strikes in the UK which paralysed the economy and led to a three-day working week. The *Penn-Ar-Bed* had capacity for 50 freight vehicles and 250 passengers and, with a service speed of 19 knots, quickly proved ideal for the six-hour crossing. She had modest public spaces including a shop, cafeteria, and an information counter, which reflected the ad hoc expansion of her passenger capacity during the building phase. On board cabin accommodation was limited and primitive by modern standards, with wire sprung beds supporting thin mattresses, underneath a low deck head.

The *Kerisnel* was transferred to Ouest Ferries, a new BAI subsidiary operating between St Nazaire and Vigo, transporting cars from the Citroën factory in Rennes for export through Galicia. This soon proved unsuccessful and closed on 26th June 1974. The *Kerisnel* was sold to Cie. Générale Maritime, Marseilles in October 1974 and renamed *La Durance*; the cash helped stabilise the Company's financial position and removed a liability from the books. Meanwhile, Hénaff was replaced as president by Gourvennec, and the Company offices moved to Roscoff.

During October Brittany Ferries chartered the 3,390-gt freight ship *Valérie*, whilst the *Penn Ar Bed* underwent her first annual survey and overhaul. The charter of a freight-only substitute proved unpopular with customers, as passenger traffic was now increasing steadily.

In the 1974 season Brittany Ferries carried 91,500 passengers, 12,483 cars, and the 9,648 freight vehicles represented a 75% rise in traffic from 1973. Turnover tripled to FF21 million on what was still a one-ship service. This growth prompted approaches from other ferry operators, including P&O's Normandy Ferries, who offered to buy a shareholding, enter a joint operation, or buy out the founding shareholders. Gourvennec and the Board were not interested in this opportunism.

The new year was accompanied by the lifting of a potential threat to the fledgling Company, when the UK government cancelled construction work on the Channel Tunnel on 20th January 1975, citing uncertainty about the country's membership of the EEC, a doubling of the project cost estimates, and general uncertainty in the economy.

An international group of trade union protesters march through the streets of St Malo. *(Ferry Publications Library)*

The *Mary Poppins* arrives in London for a publicity visit prior to heading for Southampton to inaugurate the TT-Line route to St Malo. *(Ferry Publications Library)*

Provision of a second vessel became Brittany Ferries' priority for the 1975 season. Maurice Chollet, the Company's first chief financial officer, understood that this would bring the right degree of flexibility and back up to the existing operation, whilst generating the possibility of future profit. Capacity needed to expand to create economies of scale and protect the growing volumes of traffic from competition. But there was insufficient business in the west to justify adding a second vessel to the Plymouth-Roscoff roster. A new route was needed.

The authorities in St Malo also looked on enviously at the growth of the new service; the port had not seen a year-round cross-Channel ferry service since the demise of the British Railways route to Southampton in 1964. The Malouins began to consider whether it would be possible to install a linkspan in their port to tap into the growing interest in ro-ro traffic. These ambitions coincided with Brittany Ferries' aspirations to protect their investment in Roscoff by expanding their route structure to prevent

The ***Penn-Ar-Bed*** **on the berth at Roscoff, as the** ***Prince de Bretagne*** **sails for Plymouth.** *(Ferry Publications Library)*

competitive incursion. Traffic in Roscoff did not yet justify a second ship, but St Malo represented a logical expansion, enlarging the hinterland, securing the 'west' within Brittany Ferries' control, and maintaining a geographical focus on the Brittany region. Positive discussions resulted in Gourvennec agreeing to secure funding and find a second vessel to launch a service from St Malo as soon as a linkspan could be installed. The parties agreed a deadline of the end of 1976 to complete their work.

Professional expertise was needed to manage an increasingly complex business. The shareholders were farmers, not transport professionals, and the scale of the operation was moving away from their field of expertise. Gourvennec knew the right candidate for the new post of Directeur Général and had been wooing him for some time. The appointment of the experienced logistics professional Christian Michielini in January 1975 proved to be a turning point for the Company.

Michielini was appointed as a director of BAI alongside Alexis Gourvennec as chairman, and Maurice Chollet as finance director. The role of Directeur Général focused on strategic and internal management issues for the Company, and formed an effective partnership with the chairman, which freed Gourvennec to handle relationships with the shareholders and banks and manage his own farming interests.

The immediate task was to deliver the growth plans and secure a new vessel for the St Mal expansion plans.

Christian Michielini's immediate task was to deliver the growth plans by expanding the fleet and finding a vessel for the St Malo expansion plans. In April 1975 Brittany Ferries secured a six-month charter and option

Promoting the Company – Prince Phillip meets the team at the 1976 Boat Show. *(Ferry Publications Library)*

to purchase, of the *Falster*, a 2,424-gt vessel completed in January that year by Trondheims Mekaniske Verksted in Trondheim, Norway. She was 109.7-metre-long and operated at a service speed of 19 knots with capacity for 250 cars, but just 345 passengers, making this a difficult commercial ratio to balance. Renamed the *Prince de Bretagne* - in a passing reference to the vegetable brand - her arrival enabled operation of a twice-daily Plymouth-Roscoff service during the summer 1975 season. The *Penn-Ar-Bed* took the 23:00 overnight departure daily from Plymouth, returning from Roscoff at 12:00 the next day. The *Prince de Bretagne's* daily roster saw her leave Roscoff at 23:00, returning from Plymouth at 11:00. The Plymouth service was secure, but a threat was materialising further to the east.

The *Penn-Ar-Bed* entered service with Brittany Ferries in 1974 . *(FotoFlite)*

German ferry operator TT-Line shocked Brittany Ferries in January 1975 by announcing that their vessel *Gösta Berling* - renamed the *Mary Poppins* - would re-open the route from Southampton to St Malo from 29th May 1975, initially operating six return crossings each week. The 110-metre-long vessel could accommodate 850 passengers and 120 cars, with a quality of facilities better than anything then contemplated by Brittany Ferries. The St Malo port authorities had decided to take the service on offer rather than wait for a speculative venture from Brittany Ferries; Gourvennec felt betrayed. The issues were widened by TT-Line's decision to register the *Mary Poppins* under the Cypriot flag and sail with a mostly Filipino crew; French maritime unions were quick to enter the fray.

The inaugural departure of TT-Line's *Mary Poppins* from Southampton at 23:00 on Wednesday 28th May was cancelled after access to the ship was blocked by protesting dockers in the Hampshire port. Across the Channel, thousands of farmers had already travelled from Nord-Finistère to St Malo to protest on the ship's planned arrival. Friday brought further protesters to welcome the vessel, but the second departure was also cancelled. Alexis Gourvennec and Christian Michielini were amongst the protestors. The *Mary Poppins* finally left Southampton on the evening of Friday 30th May. Access to St Malo was blocked by a steel hawser as she approached the port the following morning. The Master hailed the demonstrators and asked for permission to berth; they refused. He repeated the question and received the same response. The *Mary Poppins* sailed back to Southampton, to the accompaniment of huge cheers from the quayside. TT-Line elected to cancel the remainder of the season's sailings, and the vessel withdrawn. An existential threat had been overcome.

The St Malo authorities were angered at the thwarting of their ambitions to secure a ferry service to England and this spurred Brittany Ferries' need to accelerate their plans to serve the port. Short-term options were limited, but the *Penn-Ar-Bed* operated a trial thrice-weekly service from Plymouth to St Malo from mid-August until early October 1975. It made little commercial or geographic sense, forcing many customers to make a 'dog-leg' transit of the Channel, and illustrated that the English port for a St Malo service needed to be further east than Plymouth.

Michielini was now finding his feet in the organisation and had witnessed a baptism of fire at St Malo. He needed help if Brittany Ferries were to realise their full potential. Paul Burns joined the Company from 1st July 1975 and was appointed as the Company's first UK General Manager.

Meanwhile, the chartered *Prince de Bretagne* proved unsuitable for the passenger/vehicle mix, and she was returned to her owners at the end the season in October. Instead, Brittany Ferries asked Trondheims Mekaniske Verksted to explore options to construct a similar vessel capable of carrying more passengers. An order followed for a new ship to be built in Bergen and fitted out in Trondheim, but she was not launched until 20th June 1976 and was not to enter service until 24th May 1977.

In the meantime, the Company needed to ready itself for the opening of a St Malo service in 1976, with the urgent need to finalise the English port and secure a vessel.

A Permanent route to St Malo

Planning for a service to St Malo focussed on the efficient utilisation of a ship for the route. The basic requirement was for the vessel to operate a round trip crossing every 24 hours which, with two-hour turnarounds gave a maximum sea passage time of ten hours. Discounting Plymouth and after consideration of Weymouth and Poole, attention focussed on the then undeveloped port of Portsmouth. Commodore Shipping were already active in the Portsmouth commercial port and worked with Brittany Ferries to persuade the City Council to invest in a new ferry port. The Council had not considered operating ferries from the mudflats north of Albert Johnson Quay before they received the, but the idea of so doing was quickly developed. The capital investment of approaching £1 million carried significant risk if Brittany Ferries was the only operator, so Portsmouth City Council also approached Townsend Thoresen, who eventually agreed to open a limited seasonal operation to supplement their services from Southampton. Construction work began on an area of mudflats slightly north of Commodore Shipping's Flathouse Quay operations.

More immediately, Brittany Ferries needed a second ship to supplement the *Penn-Ar-Bed* for the 1976 summer season, whilst a larger vessel required to open the Portsmouth-St Malo route on a longer-term basis. The 1971-built *Terje Vigen* was identified as having the right speed, capacity, and accommodation for the new Portsmouth operation, and she was acquired in November 1975. The *Terje Vigen* was built by Société Nouvelle des Ateliers et Chantiers in Le Havre in 1971 to sail between Oslo and Åarhus for DA-NO Linien, making her maiden voyage on 13th May 1972. Of 5,732-gt, she was 116.6 metres long, with a service speed of 20 knots; she could carry 700 passengers accommodated in 410 cabin berths and 200 reclining seats, and 170 cars. The *Terje Vigen* was one of several similar ferries, built to an innovative design by Knud. E Hansen, that made the most of external light by featuring big picture windows; she was an expensive vessel yet featured on board furniture from IKEA. After a £1 million refit at the Meyer

The French-built *Terje Vigen* was quickly identified by Mason Shipbrokers as being the right ship to open the Portsmouth-St Malo service. *(Ferry Publications Library)*

The *Armorique* at Plymouth on her first arrival at the port. *(Ferry Publications Library)*

Werft shipyard in Papenburg, West Germany, she emerged as the *Armorique*, the ancient name of the area of Gaul between the Seine and Loire.

In late February 1976 Burns contacted Ian Carruthers, a former colleague at Hertz, and asked him to join Brittany Ferries to help start the new route to St Malo.

The *Armorique* arrived in Plymouth on 4th March 1976 and operated in freight-only mode prior to her first passenger sailing to Roscoff on 25th March. The new berth at Portsmouth was not due to be ready until June so the *Armorique* operated an early season Plymouth-St Malo link from 9th April until 16th June. Summer seasonal support for the Plymouth services was provided by the *Bonanza*, chartered from Fred. Olsen to operate from 28th May to 16th September 1976. At 3,972-gt, she was 94.7 metres long with a service speed of 19 knots. Built by Ulstein Werft AS in Ulsteinvik, Norway in 1972, she could accommodate 500 passengers and 200 cars but was designed primarily for day crossings, with limited cabin capacity. Her facilities included two self-service restaurants and a duty-free shop. She made her maiden trip to Roscoff on the 16:00 crossing from Plymouth on 27th May.

Ian Carruthers joined the company on 10th May to spearhead the new Portsmouth operation. After an intense exercise to complete the port and put shore handling arrangements in place, the *Armorique* opened the Portsmouth-St Malo service on 17th June from the newly completed ferry terminal, whilst Townsend Thoresen commenced sailings to Cherbourg with the *Viking Victory* earlier the same day. The *Armorique's* maiden departure as a passenger and car-only service left at 21:00, arriving in St Malo at 08:30 the following morning, and returning at 11:00 to arrive back in Portsmouth at 19:30. Brittany Ferries' second permanent route was up and running.,

The *Olau West* was chartered by Brittany Ferries in 1976. *(FotoFlite)*

The new service got off to a difficult start. On 5th July the *Armorique* ran aground in thick fog as she approached St Malo and was withdrawn for extensive repair. The *Bonanza* switched to the Portsmouth-St Malo route, but was soon replaced by the *Penn Ar Bed*, which had better accommodation and could achieve the schedule. The 3,100-gt *Olau West* was chartered in August to replace the *Armorique*; she had been built at Schiffbau Gesellschaft Unterweser in Bremerhaven, Germany in 1964, and sold to Olau Line in 1970. A 3,061-gt vessel, she was 97.4 metres in length and offered a service speed of 18 knots. The *Olau West* was

The ***Armorique*** **shows off her new Brittany Ferries livery to advantage as she sails from Portsmouth on her morning sailing to St Malo.** *(FotoFlite)*

substantial enough to accommodate 1,500 passengers and 165 cars but was far from ideal for the service and was chartered with some misgivings. But she soon grounded in the outer entrance to St Malo on 7th August and was withdrawn for repair. The link was temporarily closed on 10th October to enable the St Malo authorities to improve the port approaches, having carried 75,000 passengers and 18,000 cars in four months of operation.

The opening of the St Malo service met resistance from UK trade unions, who feared the loss of jobs in the established 'scheme port' of Southampton. As early as January 1976 the Transport and General Workers Union (TGWU) stated in meetings held with Paul Burns that 'Portsmouth-St Malo will not happen', based on their vested interest in protecting trade union jobs in Southampton. The TGWU were soon active in advising trade union workers at other ports, including Plymouth, of the perceived threat to dockworker employment from the new operation.

The Portsmouth-St Malo service was still constrained by the agreement with trade unions to carry only passengers and their vehicles, but this was not sustainable in the longer-term. Whilst the summer season had operated without any industrial problems, a year-round service was needed to develop the freight business, so conflict with trade unions became inevitable when the *Armorique* returned to service. When she arrived in Portsmouth from St Malo at 19:30 on 8th November with her first five freight vehicles, the port was blockaded by a picket line of over 200 dockers. Outside the port, Commercial Road, the main access road into Portsmouth, was closed by police. The

The 'Iroise Bar' on the ***Armorique.*** *(Ferry Publications Library)*

The main restaurant on board the ***Armorique.*** *(Miles Cowsill)*

The *Penn-ar-Bed* was an ideal day ship for the company but lacked cabin capacity for the overnight sailings from Roscoff and St Malo. *(FotoFlite)*

The ro-ro vessel *Normandia* was chartered by Brittany Ferries in 1979 as additional freight capacity across their route structure. *(FotoFlite)*

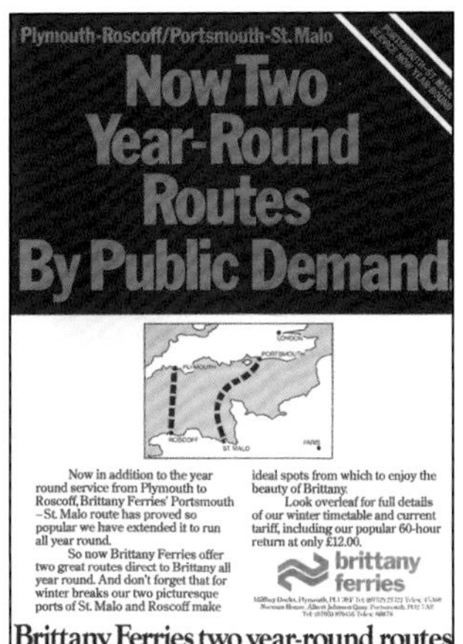

Armorique's bow door was opened at the berth, but the police advised that the load should not be discharged, so the lorries and drivers remained on board. At 21.30 Armorique departed for St Malo with her freight traffic still on board. The service was repeated the next day with the same outcome.

The following morning the *Penn-Ar-Bed* arrived in Plymouth from Roscoff loaded with 24 lorries and 52 passengers, but dockers refused to handle her in sympathy with their fellow trade union members blockading Portsmouth. The *Penn-Ar-Bed* sat outside the port throughout the day and tried again to berth in the evening but was greeted with the same refusal by the next shift of Plymouth dockers. She returned to Roscoff with her freight. Passengers were advised to drive to St Malo and cross to Portsmouth on the *Armorique*. Both routes were now being boycotted for freight movements by the TGWU dockers, and there were further trade union threats to 'black' any hauliers who used the Portsmouth-St Malo route.

This standoff continued for three weeks, with the *Armorique* operating with limited loads, eventually with agreement to discharge her payload. However, the resistance intensified, occasionally becoming violent and requiring a heavy police presence. Agreement with the trade unions was eventually reached on 30th November and the *Armorique* was able to operate as a year-round multi-purpose vessel from Portsmouth to St Malo.

This was an important and hard-won victory for Brittany Ferries. Despite being less than three years old, the Company had demonstrated its determination to succeed, whether challenged by large established operators, trade unions or 'events'. The ability to carry freight through Portsmouth laid the foundations for the future success of operations for all companies at the Continental Ferry Port. As Southampton dockers had feared, it began the demise of the cross-Channel ferry trade from their port. Ironically the big winners were those Southampton-based ferry companies who had supported and encouraged their dockers to resist Brittany Ferries' freight service. They were unashamedly quick to begin transferring their passenger and freight operations to Portsmouth after Brittany Ferries had paved the way for them to do so.

Despite all the operational problems, 1976 proved to be a successful year for Brittany Ferries, carrying 281,200 passengers, 48,261 cars, and 12,205 freight vehicles to achieve a turnover of FF60 million. The Company was beginning to make its mark.

With traffic growing and strong advance interest in the upcoming season, Brittany Ferries made plans to introduce additional sailings on both the Portsmouth-St Malo and Plymouth-Roscoff routes in 1977, and to maintain a twice-weekly schedule on the Plymouth-St Malo route. From 23rd May until 24th September 1977, the Portsmouth-St Malo route was set to enjoy two return crossings from Monday to Friday, with one return crossing on Saturdays and Sundays.

In April 1977 Christian Michielini brought Jacques le Rouzo, who had extensive catering experience with

Madame Colin, Alexis Gourvennec and Christian Michielini at the blessing ceremony for the *Cornouailles*. *(Ferry Publications Library)*

The *Cornouailles*, sporting a large Brittany Ferries logo on her bow, undertakes berthing trials at Plymouth. *(Ferry Publications Library)*

French Line, into the Company, with the brief of developing on board catering facilities to meet the needs of the British market, but with a French twist. This was the start of a culinary revolution that helped define and distinguish the Brittany Ferries product from its competitors. The shipping industry had a tradition of corruption and dubious employment practices, and France was no exception to this. The Hotel Services department on French ships was often the position of last resort for officers displaced from more technical roles. The situation in Roscoff was not helped by an

The *Penn-Ar-Bed* approaching Portsmouth whilst covering for the *Armorique* and sporting full Brittany Ferries' livery. *(FotoFlite)*

A powerful view of the *Armorique* on passage to St Malo, pictured off the Isle of Wight. *(FotoFlite)*

equivalent lack of maritime expertise in the shore management team, as Brittany Ferries grappled with the issues of an expanding business. Le Rouzo set out to change this and radically overhaul the business. He began by establishing a comprehensive set of catering and accommodation standards to be applied across the fleet and won enthusiastic support right across the Company.

Brittany Ferries' first new build vessel - the much delayed 3,383-gt *Cornouailles* - entered service from Plymouth on 24th May 1977, although she was prevented from docking at Roscoff on her maiden voyage by protesting fishermen. Such action was to punctuate operations for many years to come. The *Cornouailles* was resplendent in her white hull with a blue and orange horizontal stripe and became the first vessel to sport the new Brittany Ferries logo on her funnels – a symbolic representation of the interaction between the coasts of Brittany and southwest England. Her arrival allowed sailing frequency between Plymouth and Roscoff to be increased, with up to three a day being offered at weekends. The *Penn Ar Bed* operated twice weekly between Plymouth and St Malo and supported the *Armorique* on the Portsmouth link.

Brittany Ferries organised a publicity coup at the Spithead Fleet Review to commemorate the Silver Jubilee of HM Queen Elizabeth on 27th/28th June 1977, when the *Armorique* cruised to view the assembled ships, with 600 passengers paying £100 each to view the spectacle.

The *Cornouailles* suffered a bow thruster failure and had to be replaced by the *Penn-Ar-Bed* whilst undergoing repair. Better news came from the *Armorique*, which operated flawlessly from Portsmouth with the troubles of 1976 now well behind her.

The winter 1977-78 schedule encompassed one daily return sailing on both the Portsmouth-St Malo and Plymouth-Roscoff routes. The positive improvements in business enabled the *Penn-Ar-Bed* to be dry docked and return to service with her capacity increased to 420 passengers, expanded sleeping accommodation, and 154 new reclining seats.

When the Company was established as BAI, the name indicated an ambition to add Ireland to the route structure as part of the strategy to link the Celtic nations at the edge of Europe. Attention turned to finding a way to opening a service from Ireland to France and discussions were held with the authorities in Cork. Then came news that both Swedish Lloyd and Aznar Line were withdrawing their routes from Southampton to Bilbao and Santander respectively, leaving Spain without a direct ferry service from the UK. Was this an opportunity for Brittany Ferries?

A 424-nautical mile route from Plymouth to Santander would be significantly shorter than the 550-nautical mile crossing from Southampton. The French government allowed French-flagged ships to sail inside

The *Prince of Fundy* was acquired by Brittany Ferries in 1978. *(Ferry Publications Library)*

Ouessant, shaving the crossing length for a Brittany Ferries service by another 20 nautical miles. A Plymouth sailing could reach Spain in 24 hours, saving passengers two nights on their round-trip holiday journey compared to established Southampton routes, whilst improving vessel productivity. Further, if the vessel operated to Spain during the week, it could provide additional capacity from Plymouth to Roscoff at weekends, whilst repositioning to link Roscoff and Ireland and fulfill the Celtic dream. The Board was initially hesitant, but eventually agreed with plans to deploy the *Armorique* on the proposed intensive schedule.

If the *Armorique* was to move to Plymouth then replacement tonnage was need for the Portsmouth-St Malo route, and the *Prince of Fundy* was identified as the ideal choice. She was built in 1970 by Schiffbau Gesellschaft Unterweser AG in Germany for Lion Ferry and for the Portland, Maine-Yarmouth, Nova Scotia route until 1976, when she transferred to the Varberg-Grenå service for the 1977 season. She brought increased capacity for 1,000 passengers (300 higher than the *Armorique*) and 220 cars (50 higher) on the route. The *Prince of Fundy* offered 561 berths, 421 of which were in en suite cabins, with a further 132 in cabins with a washbasin, plus 150 reclining Pullman seats. Other facilities included a buffet restaurant, café, two bars, a disco, duty-free supermarket, and television in the reclining seat areas. Her additional capacity allowed for expansion of the St Malo route. The *Prince of Fundy* was renamed the *Prince of Brittany*.

By the end of the 1977 season, Brittany Ferries' freight traffic had grown to 16,194 vehicles, of which 25% was French agricultural produce, with expectations of 24,000 units in 1978. Passenger traffic had reached 383,536 passengers.

On to Ireland and Spain

In the winter of 1977/78, the *Armorique* undertook a cruise to Lisbon, Morocco, and the Canary Islands to test the market for a cruise product, a concept which the Roscoff team were keen to promote. But the *Armorique's* passenger accommodation was designed for short duration trips of a maximum of two nights, and her cabins did not lend themselves to delivering a genuine cruise experience. She returned to launch the new services to Ireland and Spain.

The *Armorique* left Roscoff for the Irish route inauguration celebrations on 16th March and arrived in Cork on a cold St Patrick's morning, berthing at Custom House Quay. During the evening's celebrations on board the *Armorique*, news arrived that the oil tanker *Amoco Cadiz*, was lying astride the Men Goulven rocks off the coast of Brittany with her back broken and leaking her cargo of 223,000 tonnes of crude oil. This environmental disaster, from an oil slick covering 80 miles of beaches, was accompanied by unwelcome publicity for Brittany's holiday businesses. News programmes were dominated by images of wildlife casualties and oily sand. The subsequent booking cancellations and refunds almost brought the company to bankruptcy. Alexis Gourvennec approached the French government for support, Maurice Chollet dealt with the banks, whilst the UK management team did their best to shore up the business and maintain the confidence of staff and suppliers. An urgent solution was needed to save the Company.

The Brittany tourism problem needed a British solution if the industry was to recover, as the French habitually do not go north for their annual holidays. Whilst the beaches were out of bounds, their hinterland was not tainted with contamination. There was a plentiful supply of small cottages and farmhouses that could be used for holidays that would resonate with lovers of the French lifestyle. The concept of selling gîte holidays was born, and the holiday programme was to

The *Prince of Brittany* on passage to St Malo. *(Ferry Publications Library)*

The *Armorique* on her berth at Tivoli in the heart of the city of Cork. *(Port of Cork)*

become a major component of the Brittany Ferries brand in the UK and Ireland.

Meanwhile, the *Prince of Brittany* arrived in Portsmouth on 15th April ready to take over the St Malo service, freeing the *Armorique* to transfer to Plymouth and launch the Santander service the following day. The inaugural sailing from Plymouth on 17th April featured 38 vintage Rolls Royce and Bentley cars. The season operated successfully justifying the confidence in the Company's ability to operate the complex intensive schedule.

The port of Tivoli (Cork) continued to prove to be a difficult place to operate to because of the physical constraints on access. The *Armorique* consistently hit mud as she tried to turn in the port area, and the authorities were indifferent to requests to undertake the necessary dredging. This was no way to run a ferry service and Paul Burns began to look for an alternative location.

Passengers disembark from the first arrival of the *Armorique* at Santander. *(Modesto Piñeiro collection)*

The *Breizh-Izel* leads the *Armorique* into Cork on 1st July 1979. *(Ferry Publications Library)*

Brittany Ferries' horizons were not limited to France and Spain, but opportunities to operate from Warrenpoint or Greenore across the Irish Sea to Heysham and a joint operation from Cork with Irish Continental Line were reviewed but not taken forward. An option to operate a Jetfoil service from Dieppe to Newhaven, Portsmouth, and the Channel Islands was also reviewed, but there was scepticism that the craft could meet the ambitious schedule needed to make a financial return, and the concept was not progressed.

The Brittany Regional Tourist Committee judged the 1978 season to be "the worst that the Finistère hotel industry has ever known", with visitors down by 50% up to June, 36% in July and 20% in August, and all coastal communities suffering a drastic fall, irrespective of whether they had been affected by the oil spill on the beaches. But a full year of the Portsmouth-St Malo route enabled Brittany Ferries to record substantial growth in business to 525,700 passengers, 96,328 cars and 20,618 freight vehicles – all records by some margin, although substantially less than might have been anticipated without the misfortune of the *Amoco Cadiz.*

The *Armorique* spent a lengthy autumn and winter at the Falmouth Ship Repair yard being fitted with new Sperry Gyrofin stabilisers and undergoing a major refurbishment of her passenger facilities. Trapped by a strike at the shipyard, she was unable to inaugurate the new year-round Santander and Cork season on 10th February 1979. The *Prince of Brittany* temporarily transferred to cover the Santander service, with the *Armorique's* return delayed until April.

The 1979 schedule envisaged that the Plymouth-Roscoff route would be covered by the *Cornouailles*, with the *Prince of Brittany* and *Penn-Ar-Bed* allocated to the Portsmouth-St Malo service, whilst the *Penn-Ar-Bed* operated the linking Plymouth-St Malo route. Growing freight traffic encouraged the Company to supplement the fleet by chartering the 1971-built *Normandia* for additional capacity across Channel routes, whilst also offering sailings from Roscoff to Cork. The 105.3-metre vessel could carry 480 lane-metres of freight but was only to spend a single season with Brittany Ferries.

The *Cornouailles* broke down with engine problems in mid-June and was withdrawn for repair, forcing a charter of the 4,067-gt *Munster* from B&I Line for a 20-day period. The 1,000 passenger and 220 car capacity vessel arrived in Plymouth from Roscoff on 4th July and had barely settled into her new schedule when the *Penn-Ar-Bed* and *Prince of Brittany* both suffered engine issues, forcing their withdrawal. All three had been refitted in the same shipyard at Brest the previous winter, and attention focused on the engine bearings fitted during these overhauls.

The *Munster's* charter was extended following the *Prince of Brittany's* problems, but the standards on board were poor, forcing the Company to issue multiple apologies. The *Penn-Ar-Bed* re-opened the Portsmouth-St Malo service on 19th July and the *Munster* arrived in Portsmouth on 8th August, to release the *Cornouailles* to return to Plymouth for the remainder of the summer. She briefly ran aground on her first crossing to St Malo but was able to resume her schedule as the damage was slight. Meanwhile, the 1972-built 8,020-gt *Regina* was chartered from 6th September until 1st October to cover for the *Prince of Brittany.* Irish bookings were stronger than anticipated and the *Cornouailles* replaced the *Penn-Ar-Bed* on the Cork-Roscoff service during the peak season to offer increased capacity. Meanwhile, discussions continued with B&I Line on a possible joint venture on Irish services.

By the year end Brittany Ferries had carried 618,912 passengers, 117,248 cars, and freight vehicles reached a record 25,156. Christian Michielini commented, "some said that this Company was a foolish gamble, managed by a band of idiots. I think that the figures we are making are demonstrating the contrary."

The *Prince of Brittany* received a new operating partner on the Portsmouth-St Malo route for the 1980 season. The 5,071-gt *Viking 6*, a 5,071-tonne vessel with capacity for 1,200 passengers and 215 cars, was renamed *Goelo* after the region in the northeast of

The *Viking 6* pictured on the Kapellskär-Mariehamn-Naantali route during her last season in the Baltic, prior to her charter to Brittany Ferries and renaming as the *Goelo*. *(Ferry Publications Library)*

Brittany. She chartered from Viking Line from mid-June until mid-September 1980. The *Goelo* had accommodation for 609 passengers in a combination of cabins and sleeperettes, and her facilities included two bars, a cafeteria and restaurant, and a duty-free supermarket and gift shop. She was a big step forward in standards of cabin accommodation on the English Channel, having previously been employed in the Alaskan cruise market. The *Goelo's* major disadvantage was a low deck height, which precluded her carrying significant volumes of freight traffic. She was therefore supplemented by the Italian freighter *Faraday*; she could carry 1,230 lane-metres of freight and twelve passengers. Meanwhile, the *Prince of Brittany* was purchased from her Swedish owners for $8 million and re-registered in Morlaix under the French flag.

A charter arrangement for the ten-year-old freighter *Iniochos Express* expanded capacity on the Roscoff, Santander and Cork services. She was built by the Taikoo Dockyard & Engineering Company in Hong Kong for the Union Steamship Company of Wellington, New Zealand, and was 111.6 metres in length and could carry twelve passengers and 65 freight vehicles at a service speed of 16.5 knots. The *Iniochos Express* was renamed *Breizh-Izel*, the Breton name for Lower Brittany.

Peak summer traffic was severely disrupted when French fishermen began another blockade of Channel ports on 13th August 1980, in protest at high fuel costs, falling wholesale fish prices, and plans to reduce crews and salaries. French police advised home-bound tourists to travel to Ostend and Zeebrugge to beat the blockade. 15,000 passengers were trapped in France by the dispute and tempers flared. By 19th August all

The *Munster* had an eventful summer on charter to Brittany Ferries. *(Miles Cowsill)*

The *Regina* is seen at Portsmouth during her brief spell with Brittany Ferries. *(Ferry Publications Library)*

The attractive-looking *Goelo* outward bound from Plymouth, prior to the vessel establishing herself on the St. Malo link during her two-year charter. *(Ferry Publications Library)*

Brittany Ferries purchased the *Breizh-Izel* in 1980 for freight operations within the Group. *(Ferry Publications Library)*

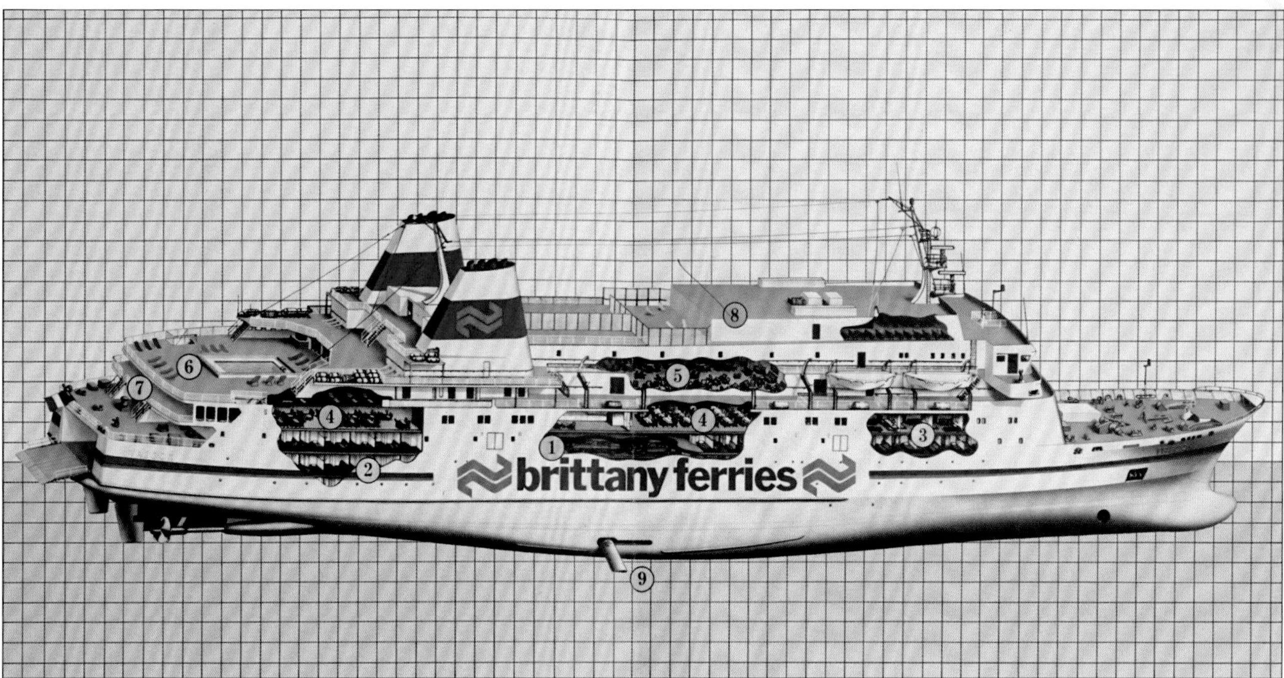

A cutway drawing of the proposed *Trégor* for the Santander service. *(Ferry Publications Library)*

French channel ports except Roscoff were blockaded, and a five-sailing schedule was planned from Portsmouth and Plymouth to serve the port. Meanwhile, angry lorry drivers blocked roads into Cherbourg in retaliation. The *Cornouailles* was prevented from leaving Roscoff on 20th August and the situation became increasingly desperate.

Unlike other ferry operators, Brittany Ferries did not have alternative Channel ports in Belgium or Holland. To provide some relief for holidaymakers, the *Armorique, Prince of Brittany* and *Goelo* transferred to sail from Plymouth to Santander, departing at 90-minute intervals on 20th August; the *Penn-Ar-Bed* followed the next day. Britany Ferries faced substantial extra fuel and crew costs at the same time as bookings were being refunded. The Company was running out of money; here was another existential crisis. Gourvennec went to Roscoff to speak to the fishermen's leaders but faced a robust response. He indicated that he would return with six muck spreaders and use them to spray the fishing fleet; he gave the fishermen one hour to clear the berth. The blockade of Roscoff was lifted and the *Cornouailles* sailed on 21st August with 200 cars and 500 stranded passengers on board. By the end of the week support for the national dispute was waning, and fishermen withdrew their blockade.

Gourvennec's robust action stopped Brittany Ferries being closed, but financial problems were exacerbated by rising costs, and the additional charter costs incurred in the expanding services to Ireland and Spain. The fragile Company could not sustain finance charges, which had reached ten per cent of turnover. Trading losses mounted to £1 million, despite an 18% rise in business and the growing success of the holiday business. Prospects for the 1981 season were bleak, with UK inflation standing at 18% and unemployment at two million.

During December Brittany Ferries announced plans to charter the Fred. Olsen ship *Bolero* (11,344-gt) and rename her *Tregor* to expand the Santander service to three sailings a week. The *Bolero* was built in 1973 by Dubegion-Normandie S.A. Prairie au doc, of Nantes as a sister to the ill-fated *Scandinavian Star*, and a near sister to Southern Ferries' *Eagle*. She was 141.2 metres in length, with a beam of 21.9 metres, and could carry 1,600 passengers in 800 cabins, with deck capacity for 245 vehicles and 22 freight units. Her service speed was 18 knots. The *Bolero* operated as the *Prince of Fundy II* in the summers of 1973 to 1976 between Portland, Maine, and Yarmouth, Nova Scotia. During the winters she operated for Commodore Cruise Lines, before transferring to Scandinavian services.

However, the plan fell through at the eleventh hour, the Company stating that the charter could not be finalised for the 1981 season. At Plymouth, the BTDB were investing over £1.1 million in a linkspan and facilities to accommodate the expanded service and the new ship, *Trégor*. Steel had been ordered in Cork to support an upgrade at Ringaskiddy; arrangements were being made in Santander. Fred. Olsen threatened to sue over the failed charter. The 1981 brochure featuring the *Trégor* had to be pulped, hastily recast, and reprinted, with schedules based on the *Armorique*. The Company had to disentangle itself from all these agreements.

This fiasco prompted the resignation of Paul Burns, who had invested much personal capital in the project. He was replaced in the UK by Ian Carruthers.

GOELO

Goelo. *(FotoFlite)*

A new financial structure

In 1981, Alexis Gourvennec was elected as Chairman of Crédit Agricole de Finistère, then the second largest to Paris of the banks that constituted the Crédit Agricole co-operative. There was still a strong desire to consider opening a route to a port further east than St Malo, to strengthen the Company's market position. In a change from the strategy that initially considered a route from Dieppe more important, Alexis Gourvennec and Christian Michielini opened discussions with the city of Caen about a new route from Portsmouth, which could open as early as 1983 and deliver up to an estimated 500,000 extra passengers, perhaps rising to as many as 1.5 million within five years. Caen had no direct competition, which made it a much more attractive proposition than Dieppe. When the discussions became public, there was a strong response from the ports of Le Havre and Cherbourg, but Alexis Gourvennec was philosophical. "The government will give some money for the new port at Caen, and some money for new roads from Cherbourg, so everyone will be happy" he said.

The *Prince of Brittany* was chartered by Irish Continental Line (ICL) prior to the start of the 1981 season, and further co-operation took place in July, when the *Breizh-Izel* was chartered for the Rosslare and Cherbourg/Roscoff services. The *Goelo* completed her final Portsmouth-St Malo crossing on 28th August and was returned to her owners at the end of her two-year charter period.

One lesson from the fallout from the *Trégor* cancellation was that further management resource was needed to support the drive for growth from the UK if plans for further expansion were to be realised. The structure was just too lean. Carruthers moved quickly to find support, returning to one his colleagues at Hertz and Heron and bringing David Longden into the Company.

Further financial problems were evident when Brittany Ferries announced 1981 losses of £2.4 million, caused by heavy borrowings to acquire the *Prince of Brittany* and the *Breizh-Izel*, and a price war depressing income on the English Channel services. It was clear

The German-built *Nils Dacke* was chartered by Brittany Ferries in 1982 for the Santander and Cork operations in place of the *Armorique*. The Swedish ship was renamed *Quiberon* for her new role and later purchased by the Company. *(Ferry Publications Library)*

The *Quiberon* dressed overall on her first visit to Roscoff, prior to opening the Spanish and Irish services. *(FotoFlite)*

that the Company could not continue to rely on chartering elderly secondhand tonnage if it was to be a major competitor in the cross-Channel market. Significant investment was needed. Gourvennec looked to the French government for help, but the proposed conditions proved onerous. He mobilised Breton resources behind a new regionally based rescue plan. The outcome was an elegant and very French financial solution. A Société d'Économie Mixte (SEM) was established to borrow money and purchase vessels at market rates, which it would own and charter back to Brittany Ferries, thereby providing capital and financial credibility for the Company. In return, Brittany Ferries would fund the interest on capital loaned to the SEM by paying agreed market-rate charter fees over a fixed duration. The outcome was the creation of the Société Anonyme Bretonne d'Économie Mixte d'Équipement Naval (Sabemen), whose founding shareholders were the Brittany Region, the Brittany départements, the Pays de Loire Region, and Brittany Ferries. This was a pivotal moment for the Company.

The rescue package was ratified by the Breton Regional Council in February 1982. Ownership of the *Armorique, Cornouailles* and *Prince of Brittany* was transferred to Sabemen, and they were immediately chartered back to Brittany Ferries, which benefited from an £8.5 million cash injection. The Company now had the solid financial backing to make the right fleet decisions and invest appropriately.

This firm financial footing prompted further expansion and development. A new office block was built at Portsmouth to handle operations and administration of the gite and holiday packages. Meanwhile, a ten-year agreement with the British Transport Docks Board (BTDB) gave the company exclusive berthing rights at the Plymouth ferry terminal. The BTDB agreed in turn to improve port facilities.

With increased demand across the company's routes, especially on the Santander service, Brittany Ferries chartered, with an option to purchase, the 7,950-gt *Nils Dacke*. The ship could sail at 22.5 knots, thereby enabling a potential two-hour reduction in peak crossing times on the Spanish route. The 7,950-gt, 129.0-metre-long ship could carry 1,140 passengers accommodated in 757 berths in 280 cabins. Her car deck accommodated 252 cars, although her freight capacity was restricted. She could replace the *Armorique* on the Irish and Spanish services, allowing her to transfer back to her original Portsmouth-St Malo route. But the *Breizh-Izel* would have to work in tandem with the new acquisition to top-up freight capacity to Santander. The *Nils Dacke* was renamed *Quiberon*, after the peninsula and town in southern Brittany, and went for an extensive refit at Jos. L. Meyer's shipyard at Papenburg, where spare space on her upper car deck (Deck 5) was converted to cabin accommodation to give her a cruise ferry configuration. Her main passenger facilities were located on Deck 6, where she

The *Quiberon* makes an impressive sight off the western coast of Brittany between the Pointe du Raz and the Île de Sein on passage from Spain to England. Today the vessels no longer take this passage. *(Ferry Publications Library)*

The *Viking 1* was chartered for the St Malo link following the fire on board the *Prince of Brittany.* *(Ferry Publications Library)*

Local Roscoff residents greet the *Quiberon* on her first arrival at the French port. *(Ferry Publications Library)*

featured an à la carte restaurant (Le Sinagot), a self-service restaurant (Les Îles), Le Ponant Café, and the tearoom Le Moulin Mer, together with two gift shops. Two small cinemas could be found on deck 5, together with a kiosk and perfume shop. The *Quiberon* entered service in May, allowing the *Armorique* to return to the Portsmouth-St Malo route. The *Quiberon* covered the Cork service at weekends and operated additional summer sailings between Plymouth and Roscoff.

The *Prince of Brittany* suffered a serious fire during the early spring, which destroyed her generators. Sealink's *Ailsa Princess* was drafted to cover the St Malo route, until the 4,485-gt *Viking 1* could be chartered from Rederi AB Sally, prior to the return of the *Prince of Brittany* to service on 14th May. Meanwhile, the *Armorique* joined the 'Prince' from 20th May until the end of September. This roster formed the basis of operations until 1988, allowing the *Prince of Brittany* to sail from St Malo in the morning and the *Armorique* overnight to Portsmouth. The winter service comprised of one sailing a day from each port.

Just before the end of the *Armorique's* 1982 summer season, she again became a victim of the treacherous approaches to St Malo, grounding during thick fog on 18th September. She was withdrawn from service for repair and the now sale-listed *Penn Ar Bed* returned to cover the rest of her season. On the return of the *Armorique*, the *Prince of Brittany* operated a one-off cruise by the company between Le Havre, Cork, and Swansea during October.

By the autumn of 1982, the Company was well on the road to financial recovery and exploited the public relations opportunities arising from the raising of the

Prince of Brittany *(FotoFlite)*

Henry VIII warship *Mary Rose* in the Solent on 11th October. The Carruthers *Prince of Brittany* was taken out of service for two days to be chartered by the Mary Rose Trust as host vessel for VIPs witnessing the event. The raising of the vessel was also broadcast live on BBC television. Jacques Le Rouzo arranged for the Company's best chefs to be on board to feed the 400 guests of the Trust and British Petroleum, one of the main sponsors. Also amongst the VIP guests on board were Prince Charles, King Constantine of Greece, Lord Mountbatten of Romsey, and the Earl of Marchwood.

The 1982 season ended with further growth recorded to reach 749,386 passengers, but the difficult trading conditions were evident in slight falls in passenger vehicles (to 136,612) and freight units (to 24,230). However, the pound sterling was trading well against the French Franc, hitting a peak of FF12 before slipping back slightly in the autumn. This provided a further boost to corporate finances.

The Brittany Centre opened at Portsmouth at the start of 1983, and in the spring the company also commissioned a new linkspan at the port, suitable for ferries up to 15,000-gt. Meanwhile, before the summer season, more than £1 million was spent upgrading the passenger facilities on the *Quiberon*, *Prince of Brittany* and *Armorique*. The *Armorique* covered the *Quiberon's* duties on the Plymouth roster whilst she was away at refit. It was to be an eventful exchange. As the *Armorique* headed on her outward journey from Roscoff to Cork at around 05:00 on 2nd April 1983, fire

was detected in a linen cupboard forward on deck 5. The vessel was around 20 miles north of the Isles of Scilly, with 680 passengers on board at the time. The blaze lasted for about an hour before being out by the *Armorique's* crew, but generators on board were put out of action. The *Armorique* was eventually escorted to Mount's Bay by the St. Mary's lifeboat and the *St. Killian,* arriving there early in the afternoon.

Sadly, one passenger died, eleven were admitted to hospital and 67 were seen and subsequently discharged from the hospital emergency department, largely suffering from the effects of smoke inhalation. More than 66 cabins were found to have been damaged by smoke from the fire. The subsequent investigation revealed that a group of French schoolchildren had

The *Apollo* pictured at Kapellskär during her last season in the Baltic with Viking Line, prior to her sale to Olau Line as the *Olau Kent* in 1976. After operations on the North Sea and a further short period in the Baltic as the *Gelting Nord*, she was chartered to Brittany Ferries in 1983 and became the *Bénodet*. *(Ferry Publications Library)*

The ***Bénodet*** **was chartered in 1983 to increase the capacity on the Roscoff-Plymouth service. She remained on the link for just over a year before opening a new route to the Channel Islands in a joint venture between Brittany Ferries, Huelin-Renouf and MMD.** *(FotoFlite)*

started the fire as a prank, following several previous attempts to start a blaze.

Passenger volumes broke through the 750,000 level for the first time in 1983, reaching 755,316, and there was a slight recovery in the number of passenger vehicles to 140,413, and freight units to 24,302.

On 31st December 1983, Townsend Thoresen finally closed their Southampton passenger operation and transferred all their western Channel passenger services to Portsmouth. The Solent port had been the company's home since the start of the Thoresen Car Ferries operation.

Summer schedules for 1984 were largely unchanged, although the *Breizh-Izel* was introduced on the Santander route to support the *Quiberon*. The Danish-registered 4,371-gt *Gelting Nord* was chartered for the Plymouth-Roscoff service in place of the *Cornouailles*. One of four sisters built by Meyer Werft in the 1970s, the vessel started life as the *Apollo*, operating for Viking Line between Kapellskär in Sweden, and Mariehamn and Nädendan in Finland, before being sold to Nordisk Færgefart and renamed *Gelting Nord*. She was 108.7 metres in length and could carry 1,200 passengers and 260 cars at 18.5 knots. Brittany Ferries had limited experience of operating her sister, *Viking 1*, during the disruption to service caused by the *Prince of Brittany* fire in 1982. She was renamed the *Bénodet* after the resort in Southern Brittany and entered service on 30th April. The *Benodet* was a major improvement over the *Cornouailles*, with more space for cars and superior cabin and passenger accommodation.

The *Bénodet* had a successful first season and was sent to St Malo for further refit work in the autumn. The

The *Breizh-Izel* proved a reliable freight workhorse for the Company. *(Ferry Publications Library)*

Brittany Ferries secured a three-year bareboat charter of the Yugoslav *Njegos* in 1984. The vessel is seen here as the *Travemünde* as orginially built for German ferry operations. *(Ferry Publications Library)*

The German-built ***Trégastel*** shows her clean lines as she gets underway from Plymouth during her first season on the Roscoff route. Note the funnel logo has been incorrectly applied in reverse. *(Ferry Publications Library)*

The passenger area between the dining room and bar on the *Trégastel*. *(Ferry Publications Library)*

Dressed overall for Bastille Day, the *Armorique* heads out of Portsmouth on her nine-hour sailing to St Malo. *(Miles Cowsill)*

Penn-Ar-Bed, which had been laid up since her period covering for the *Armorique* on the Portsmouth-St Malo route, was brought back into service on the winter Plymouth-Roscoff service when the *Cornouailles* headed for Newhaven in January.

Brittany Ferries experienced a small drop in tourist carryings in 1984, with passenger volumes falling by 3.2% to 731,422 and vehicles by 4.8% to 133,711, but freight traffic continued to grow with a rise of 11.8% to 27,162 units. With the pound sterling holding steady at an exchange rate of above FF11 throughout the year and prospects for the 1985 season of continued stability, corporate income was at the highest levels since Brittany Ferries had been established.

The option to purchase the *Quiberon* was exercised in December 1984, and she was bought for FF97.3 million supported by public aid of FF8.4 million, following two very successful seasons on the Santander

The *Trégastel* entered service on the Plymouth-Roscoff service in 1985.
(FotoFlite)

and Cork services. The *Prince of Brittany* was refurbished during the winter period with attention to her cabins, increased seating provision in the cafeteria and a new reclining seat area. The *Bénodet* was allocated to a new Channel Islands link from March 1985, so the Company secured a three-year bareboat charter of the Yugoslav ferry 3,998-gt *Njegos*. She had been built in 1971 by Schiffau-Gesellschaft Unterweser in Bremerhaven and formerly operated as the *Travemünde* between Gedser and Travemünde. The 3,999-gt vessel offered capacity for 1,200 passengers and 370 cars, and at 20.5 knots offered greater operational resilience than the *Bénodet*. She had 260 berths, predominantly in two-berth cabins, and reclining seat accommodation for 400 passengers. On board facilities included a 300-seat self-service coffee shop, a 200-seat restaurant, a children's playroom, bar duty-free supermarket and a gift shop. The *Njegos* was renamed the *Trégastel*, after the commune in the Côtes-d'Armor department in Brittany. Her arrival would bring a doubling of capacity on the Plymouth-Roscoff route in just two years. The *Trégastel* was sent to the Meyer Werft shipyard at Papenburg for a £750,000 refurbishment programme prior to her delivery, which included the fitting of a new reclining seat area. She entered service on the Plymouth-Roscoff service on 1st May 1985; prior to her arrival, the *Armorique* had covered the link following the transfer of the *Bénodet*.

The *Cornouailles* was chartered to SNCF in 1984 for their Newhaven-Dieppe service. *(Miles Cowsill)*

A very striking view of the *Quiberon* as she arrives at Santander. *(Ferry Publications Library)*

Opening to Caen

Plans for easterly expansion in France to serve Normandy were a long time in gestation, with Brittany Ferries working closely with the region to facilitate implementation of a route from Portsmouth to Caen. Such a route would bisect Townsend Thoresen's established services to Le Havre and Cherbourg and take advantage of the growing French autoroute network. Townsend Thoresen were not interested in serving the port, so the way was clear for Brittany Ferries to establish a unique link. The city lay inland, linked to the sea by the Caen canal, so an efficient service required the terminal to be close to the mouth of the canal at Ouistreham. A £25 million investment in port facilities at Ouistreham was duly announced in January 1985, having been ratified by the French government. A new mixed economy company, the Société d'Équipement Naval du Calvados (Senacal) was constituted on 10th June 1985. As with the Breton model, the new SEM would acquire vessels and charter them back to Brittany Ferries at full commercial market rates. The primary shareholders of Senacal were the Basse Normandie region, the Calvados département, Brittany Ferries, the City of Caen, and the Caen Chamber of Commerce.

The establishment of the Senacal enabled the *Prinses Beatrix* to be purchased from the Zeeland Steamship Company (SMZ) to facilitate the new route. The *Prinses Beatrix* was purpose-built in 1978 for the SMZ Hoek of Holland-Harwich route. A two-class vessel, she was 131 metres long and could carry 1,500 passengers by night and 1,000 by day, together with 320 cars at a speed of 21 knots. She was already operating on a long overnight crossing, with a daytime return, so was highly suitable for the characteristics of the new Ouistreham route. The *Prinses Beatrix* was formally acquired from SMZ on 1st October 1985 for FF101.8 million (supported by public aid of FF10.1 million). The 13,505-gt vessel would become the

The *Prinses Beatrix* was purchased by Brittany Ferries in 1985 to open the new service between Portsmouth and Caen. *(Ferry Publications Library)*

The *Armorique* was chartered to SMZ as part of the purchase package for the *Prinses Beatrix*, pictured in the background sailing in tandem on the Hoek of Holland-Harwich service in 1986. *(FotoFlite)*

The *Armorique* visits the city of Caen in September 1985 with a full complement of travel trade personnel on board. *(Ferry Publications Library)*

The *Cotentin* at Cherbourg early in her career with Truckline. *(Ferry Publications Library)*

biggest ship in the fleet, and the largest ferry to operate from Portsmouth. The *Prinses Beatrix* was chartered back to SMZ to continue serving the Hoek of Holland-Harwich route until the arrival of her replacement, the *Koningin Beatrix*.

Then came news of Brittany Ferries' acquisition of Truckline's Poole-Cherbourg service and its two vessels *Coutances* and *Purbeck*. The freight operator had been established from Poole in 1973 but was struggling to compete in the cutthroat cross-Channel market. Absorption of the company helped assuage the Cherbourg authorities, who saw Brittany Ferries' forthcoming expansion of services to Caen as a threat to their established routes to Portsmouth and Poole.

Actions taken to manage pricing in advance of the 1985 summer season helped business recover from the falls of 1984, with growth of 19.5% in passengers to 873,728, and 13.9% in vehicles to 152,312, and a mammoth 211.8% growth in freight to reach 84,694 units, the latter boosted by the Truckline acquisition. In a single year, Brittany Ferries had been transformed into a significant player in the cross-Channel freight market and prospects for the 1986 season looked good.

During March and April 1986, the *Armorique* was chartered to SMZ, leaving the Dutch side of the operations on the Hoek of Holland-Harwich service in the hands of two Brittany Ferries ships. The *Prinses Beatrix* underwent a major refit in the Netherlands following completion of her charter to SMZ and was renamed the *Duc de Normandie*. The French design company AIA were appointed to redesign her interior passenger areas to reflect a taste of France. This was the start of a highly successful partnership which saw

The *Coutances* undergoing her jumboisation in 1986. This view shows her after a new central section has been inserted in the original hull. *(Ferry Publications Library)*

The crew of the *Duc de Normandie* pictured at Ouistreham prior to her first commercial sailing to Portsmouth. *(Ferry Publications Library)*

The *Due de Normandie* arrives at Portsmouth for the first time escorted by naval tugs. *(Ferry Publications Library)*

The Honfleur Restaurant located on Deck D of the *Duc de Normandie*. *(Miles Cowsill)*

Le Jardin de Monet Bar located on Deck 6 of the *Duc de Normandie*. *(Miles Cowsill)*

the designer help establish the distinctive on-board branding of the Company.

Building awareness in advance of the new Caen service, the *Armorique* made two round trips from Portsmouth to launch the route to the travel trade, travelling along the 14-kilometre canal to the Calvados capital.

The Cherbourg authorities supported Brittany Ferries' acquisition of Truckline and were offered the prospect of a passenger service on the Poole-Cherbourg route. Introducing this operation from the 1986 summer season placed pressure on Sealink British Ferries' established service from Weymouth to Cherbourg, whilst tapping into latent demand from the affluent hinterland of Poole and Bournemouth. The plan envisaged the *Coutances* and *Purbeck* continuing to operate as freight-only vessels, with the surplus *Cornouailles* offering additional twice-daily seasonal freight capacity whilst testing the passenger market potential with a summer service carrying a maximum of 300 passengers on each sailing. The crossings would feature a value-for-money approach, inspired by the 'Les Routiers' brand of restaurants in Europe, with substantially lower fares than competitors. This styling reflected the more limited services available on the vessel and helped differentiate her from the rest of the Brittany Ferries fleet. Prior to her transfer, the *Cornouailles* operated a freight-only service between Portsmouth and Caen in advance of the route's passenger operations.

Brittany Ferries took delivery of the *Prinses Beatrix* on 1st May 1986 and sent her to dry dock in Rotterdam for a refit which included conversion to a one-class

ship. Bernard Bidault of *Architectes Ingénieurs Associés* (AIA), was appointed to undertake the design, the start of an enduring and productive partnership which embraced not just the on-board design but extended to terminal and building works as well. The AIA designs on *Duc de Normandie* included a French-style patisserie with café furniture and rustic signage, a Brasserie restaurant, and a cafeteria resembling a French motorway service station. Michel Maraval was appointed Project Manager for the transformation.

The *Duc de Normandie* represented a revolution in standards, inaugurating a new generation of vessels. For the first time the interior of a Brittany Ferries vessel had been designed with passenger aesthetics and wellbeing in mind. The restaurants, public areas, retail facilities, integrated bakery, all featured décor designed to bring an immediate taste of France to the British traveller. The Claude Monet salon included a Calvados still; the wine bar had a cider press.

The *Duc de Normandie* entered service on 5th June 1986 on the 23:30 sailing from Portsmouth and Caen. She operated three crossings each day during the summer, with no Monday afternoon sailing from Portsmouth so that her schedule placed the weekend sailings in a consistent configuration to meet the peaks in outbound and return traffic. By the peak season, the freight ships *Coutances* and *Purbeck* were drafted in to assist the *Duc de Normandie*, by carrying freight at weekends. In early winter, the *Prince of Brittany* was re-scheduled from her St Malo service on Sundays, to offer one round sailing on the Caen route to move the growing freight and passenger traffic.

The 1986 season proved to be a defining step forward for Brittany Ferries. By the end of October Brittany Ferries was able to announce that they had broken through the one million passenger level for the first time in the previous twelve months. The addition of a partial year's carryings on the Portsmouth-Caen route and the opening of the Poole-Cherbourg passenger service helped passenger volumes grow by a healthy 34.8% to hit 1,117,886 passengers. Vehicle carryings recorded a 61.1% rise to reach 245,352, and there was growth of 15.9% in freight traffic to 98,176 units. This strong response prompted Brittany Ferries to consider plans to extend the 'Duc's carrying capacity by cutting the ship horizontally in two to give her a new upper car deck to meet anticipated demand, but the plans came to naught.

The growth in traffic experienced following the

The *Duc de Normandie* established the Caen route for Brittany Ferries in 1986. This view shows her leaving the port in the buoyed channel which at low water has mud flats to either side for some considerable distance. *(Miles Cowsill)*

An artist's impression of the *Bretagne*. *(Ferry Publications Library)*

acquisition of Truckline, the opening of the Portsmouth-Caen service, and the introduction of a passenger vessel to the Poole-Cherbourg route in 1986, coupled with the sound financial backing available from the SEMs, brought Brittany Ferries to the unaccustomed position of being able to contemplate the implementation of an unconstrained fleet strategy.

Demand was also growing on the Santander route. In the absence of any suitable second-hand tonnage and in a sign of long-term confidence in the route, Brittany Ferries invited tenders for a new purpose-built ferry to serve the route. There were significant internal and external political pressures to award the contract to a French shipyard, but this was still a price-sensitive decision. Competitive proposals were received from Van der Giessen de Noord in the Netherlands, and British Shipbuilders of Govan, with the lowest bid coming from the latter with a quoted price of FF437 million. Negotiations edged towards agreement with the Scottish bidders, but Sabemen had difficulty in contemplating or justifying support for investment outside France. Then the Chantiers de l'Atlantique (Alstom) shipyard in Saint-Nazaire expressed an interest in building the *Bretagne*. After further French government intervention, agreement was eventually reached to build the vessel in Saint-Nazaire at the Scottish price. The decision prompted substantial political criticism in the UK, but the contract was signed on 9th June 1987, with completion timed to allow the *Bretagne* to enter service for the 1989 summer season.

The new vessel was ordered by Sabemen and chartered to Brittany Ferries for 20 years. The new 24,534-gt vessel would offer cruise-liner standards for 2,000 passengers, with berths for just over half the passengers in two and four-berth cabins, and space for 600 cars. The ship would also boast 500 reclining seats in a special Club Lounge, a 250-seater à la carte restaurant, a 430-seat coffee shop, plus a 150-seat Croissanterie, two bars, a 150-seat wine bar, conference room, a duty-free supermarket, and an arcade of boutiques. The *Bretagne* was to be powered by four 12-cylinder Wärtsilä diesels, giving a projected service speed of 21 knots, sufficient to maintain schedules on the Spanish route in most weather conditions.

During the winter, the *Breizh-Izel* was chartered to sister company British Channel Island Ferries (BCIF) to provide the extra capacity now required on the Channel Island services, following the failure of the joint venture with Sealink and the latter's withdrawal from the routes.

There were still problems in delivering a consistent quality of on-board service, and the issue was resolved by the creation of a new subsidiary company, the Société De Services De Restauration et D'Hotellerie, or Serestel, a hotel services company bringing together all aspects of on-board service delivery. Serestel had an inspirational leader in Jacques le Rouzo, who had Christian Michielini's full backing to make whatever changes were needed to transform the organisation.

An artist's impression of the main reception area on the ***Bretagne***. It is interesting to compare this view with that on page 60. *(Ferry Publications Library)*

With a new vessel on order, the *Duc de Normandie* setting new quality standards for English Channel services, and Serestel beginning to make an impact, the corporate strapline was updated from 'The Holiday Ferry' to 'The Holiday Fleet' to provide a more accurate reflection of the on-board experience

Operations for 1987 followed the pattern of previous years, with the *Quiberon* and *Tregastel* covering the western sector of operations, the *Prince of Brittany* and the *Armorique* covering the St Malo service and the *Duc de Normandie* and freight vessel *Purbeck* sailing on the Caen route. With growing Irish and French passenger trade, Brittany Ferries reached agreement with Swansea Cork Ferries to charter the *Celtic Pride* for one round trip each week during the peak season, to offer extra capacity in addition to the *Quiberon's* weekend sailing; this arrangement was repeated in 1988.

In May the *Trégastel* returned following a major refit, during which a new fin-stabiliser system was fitted to replace the previous system. Passenger facilities were improved, with a new bar area designed by Bernard Bidault presenting a 'French village square' atmosphere. Seating and the duty-free shopping facilities were also upgraded.

The 1987 season saw further growth with new records again set across all three markets, but tourist growth was rather less than might have been anticipated given the performance of the previous year and a full season of operation of the Portsmouth-Caen route. The year was described as the nadir in British travel to France. Passenger volumes rose by 6.0% to 1,248,952, vehicles by 4.8% to 257,190 and freight units

Swansea-Cork Ferries' ***Celtic Pride*** provided useful additional capacity on the French/Irish service, she is seen here leaving Cork. She was manned by a Polish crew. *(Ferry Publications Library)*

The ***Purbeck*** is seen at Sandbanks leaving Poole en route for Cherbourg. *(Ferry Publications Library)*

The *Duc de Normandie* opened the new Caen link on 5th June 1986. *(FotoFlite)*

Brittany Ferries

The *Gotland* was chartered in 1988 for the Portsmouth-Caen service to offer additional capacity for both passenger and freight traffic. *(Miles Cowsill*

The *Cornouailles* in Truckline colours whilst operating the 'Les Routiers' Poole-Cherbourg link. *(FotoFlite)*

The *Quiberon* at Roscoff during the expansion programme of the harbour to enable the port to handle increased traffic. *(Ferry Publications Library)*

by 15.2% to 113,113, the first time that the 100,000 level had been breached in the freight sector. The additional freight capacity provided on the Portsmouth-Caen route proved highly beneficial, and with many summer sailings of the *Duc de Normandie* operating full and turning away traffic, it was clear that additional capacity would be needed if the route's longer-term potential was to be realised. Plans were announced for second ship on the Portsmouth-Caen route in 1988, to run opposite to the *Duc de Normandie* from 19th May to 11th September. The *Cornouailles* had enjoyed another successful season on the Les Routiers Poole-Cherbourg service, and her 1988 operating season was extended to run from 27th May to 11th September, with two return sailings on four days each week and one on the remaining three.

Summer 1988 also saw the bareboat charter of the Yugoslav-built ship *Gotland*, which could offer accommodation for 1,200 passengers, to supplement the *Duc de Normandie* on the Portsmouth-Caen route. The *Gotland* was built in 1973 for *Stena Line* but was sold shortly after launch to *Rederi A.B Gotland* and then chartered out to *TT-Line* and *Moby Lines*. At 123.8 metres in length and 20.5 metres beam, she could carry 1,670 passengers and 300 cars, offering similar capacity to the *Duc de Normandie*. Her interiors were distinctively Scandinavian, with designer furniture and an emphasis on bright orange fittings. Proposals to rename her the *Lisieux* were not implemented.

The *Gotland* was not planned to enter service until May, but industrial action by P&O European Ferries and Sealink crews brought chaos to English Channel services prompting the Swedish-flagged vessel to be

Top: **The *Connacht* was purchased by Brittany Ferries in 1988 for the St Malo service as part of the company's £70 million fleet renewal programme.** *(Ferry Publications Library)*

Above: **The former B&I Line vessel is seen here as the *Duchesse Anne* following her extensive refit.** *(FotoFlite)*

Duchesse Anne *(FotoFlite)*

brought into service early to convey school parties and freight between Portsmouth and Caen. The *Armorique* was also brought into service early to cover the St Malo route, while the *Prince of Brittany* was transferred to the Portsmouth-Caen service to operate passenger sailings alongside the *Duc de Normandie* and *Gotland*. By late spring when the *Breizh-Izel* was added to the roster, there were four ships on the six-hour crossing at one time. Once normal services resumed, the Portsmouth-Caen link returned to the regular two-ship passenger operation, but the freighter *Gabrielle Wehr* was chartered for the summer season to support the Portsmouth-Caen service.

The *Gotland* was sub-chartered to SNCF in late September to cover the Newhaven-Dieppe service, then to ICL and Belfast Car Ferries on the Irish Sea prior to completing her charter to Brittany Ferries at the end of 1988.

The addition of chartered tonnage on the Portsmouth-Caen route and the impact of the NUS strike on P&O European Ferries' services at Dover helped boost traffic figures. Brittany Ferries experienced dramatic growth of 36.0% in passengers to 1,698,207, in vehicles of 52.5% to 392,220, and in freight of 33.9% to reach 151,429. In the main summer season between June and September the average growth on all English Channel services in the passenger market was 4.2% and 8.7% for vehicles, but Brittany Ferries could demonstrate growth of 39.6% and 50.6% respectively.

A more permanent solution was needed to balance capacity on the Portsmouth-Caen route. Brittany Ferries purchased the B&I ferry *Connacht* to become the principal ship on the St Malo route for 1989 to run alongside the *Armorique* and release the *Prince of Brittany* to become the second vessel on the Caen service. The *Connacht* was originally built for B&I in 1978 for the Cork-Pembroke Dock route. She could offer capacity for 1,350 passengers and 316 cars and could deliver a service speed of 20 knots, making her an ideal configuration for the St Malo route. Her capacity would represent a significant step up from the 1,000 passenger, 200 car carryings of the *Prince of Brittany*.

The Company took delivery of the *Connacht* on 3rd October, to allow her to be brought up to match the fleet standards and she went to the Meyer Werft shipyard in Papenburg for a £2 million refit. The vessel was in a poor state of repair after her Irish ownership, and the eventual cost of the refurbishment proved to be twice the original estimate. Cabin accommodation was restored on 'C' deck, having only been removed by B&I Line the previous year. The cafeteria was rebuilt with high-tech equipment and 250 new seats, in preparation for a new upgraded menu to be introduced when she entered service in April 1989. A new 70-seat Viennoisserie followed the successful pattern

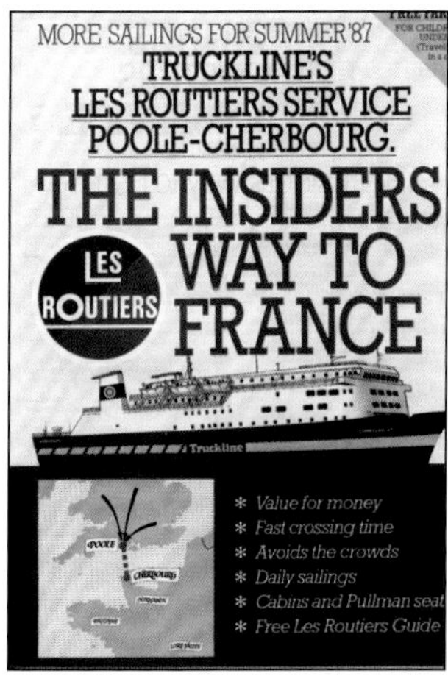

established on the *Duc de Normandie* in serving croissants and pastries. The work was completed in mid-December and the freshly named *Duchesse Anne* was chartered to Crown Line (formerly SMZ) to cover the Hoek of Holland-Harwich service. The *Prince of Brittany* remained on the St Malo route until 30th December 1988, prior to a major refit and taking up her new role. She was sold to the SEM Senacal towards the end of the year and re-registered in Caen. The *Tregastel* supported the *Duc de Normandie* on the Portsmouth-Caen service whilst the *Prince of Brittany* was away during the winter, with the *Cornouailles* transferred to the Plymouth-Roscoff route to cover for her.

The *Celtic Pride* made her final sailing for the Company in January and returned to Swansea-Cork Ferries. The *Armorique* re-opened the Plymouth-Santander service from 15th January whilst the *Quiberon* covered the refit of the *Duc de Normandie* on the Portsmouth-Caen route. BCIF returned the *Corbière* from charter and she transferred to the Poole-Cherbourg service from 26th May. Meanwhile, the *Breizh-Izel* was sold to the Marelite Marine Co. Ltd, of Limassol, Cyprus and converted to a passenger vessel as the renamed *Duchess M*.

Further investment plans were disclosed in the autumn, with the installation of a new £3.5 million computer reservations system at the Brittany Centre in Portsmouth. This enabled booking times to be shortened and became the most modern ferry reservation system in Britain.

The *Prince of Brittany* was withdrawn from the Portsmouth-St Malo route on 30th December to be given a major overhaul and refit at the Meyer Werft shipyard in Papenburg, Germany in preparation for her new role. She was sold to Senacal towards the end of 1988 and re-registered in Caen.

Early in 1989 the French government opened discussions with Brittany Ferries on the possible acquisition of the SNCF Armement Naval, the ferry arm of the nationalised state railway, which at that time operated the Newhaven-Dieppe route in partnership

Two views of the *Bretagne* as work advances on her during the winter of 1988 prior to her being floated out of the dry-dock at Saint-Nazaire. *(Patrick Depelsenaire/Chantiers de l'Atlantique)*

Bretagne - Interior concept design

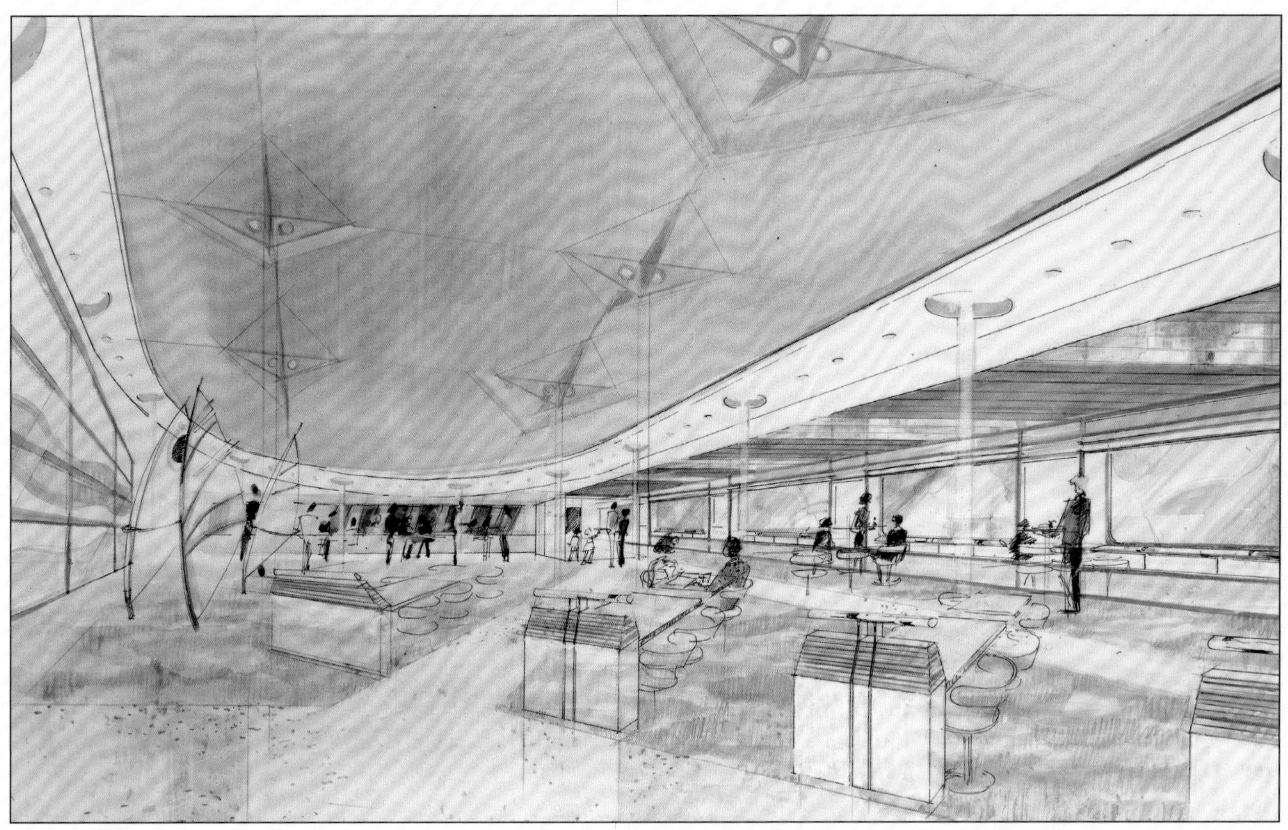

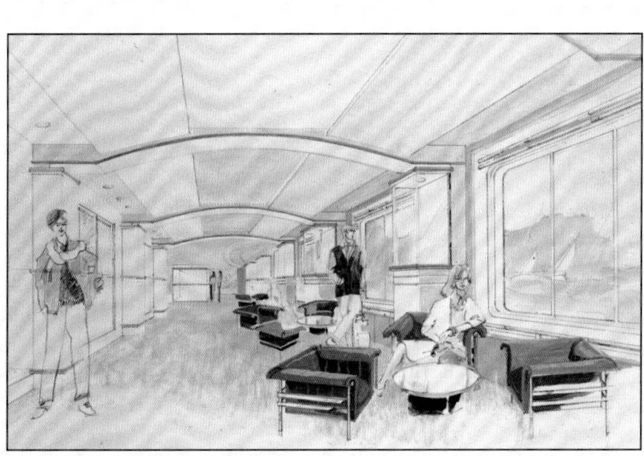

The ***Normandie Shipper*** **arrives at Portsmouth on her mid-morning sailing from Caen.** *(Miles Cowsill)*

The *Trégastel* seen shortly before taking up Truckline operations. *(Miles Cowsill)*

with Sealink British Ferries under the Sealink Dieppe Ferries brand. The operation was offered in its entirety for a knockdown price but came complete with its vessels and labour force; the opportunity was not taken up.

The arrival of the *Duchesse Anne* enabled a significant fleet re-shuffle in 1989. The *Duc de Normandie* was joined on the Portsmouth-Caen service by the former *Prince of Brittany*, which was renamed *Reine Mathilde* after William the Conqueror's queen for her new role; she made her passenger debut on 17th March. Further freight capacity was provided by the newly chartered Truckline vessel *Normandie Shipper*. The St Malo route became seasonal, running from mid-February to mid-November; the *Duchesse Anne* opened the link on 13th February, and was joined in May by the *Armorique* for an extended two-ship summer service. The *Quiberon* returned to the Plymouth-Santander route during February, after the *Armorique* had re-opened the 23-hour link on 15th January. She maintained the Santander, Roscoff and Cork services until delivery of the *Bretagne*, and then become the main vessel on the Plymouth-Roscoff route, replacing the *Tregastel* which would transfer to operate on the Poole-Cherbourg service. Delays to the *Bretagne's* delivery forced the charter of the *Corbière* (ex *Benodet*) from BCIF to open the Poole-Cherbourg season.

The 1973-built ro-ro freight vessel *Normandie Shipper* was secured on charter for three years from May 1989 and started her Portsmouth-Caen operations on 26th May. She was 142.3 metres long and could carry 1,050 lane-metres of freight traffic (equivalent to 68 x 12-metre trailers) with 36 drivers at a speed of 18 knots. Her arrival allowed the *Coutances* to return from Portsmouth to join sister *Purbeck* on the Truckline Poole-Cherbourg link.

The £55 million *Bretagne* was launched at St Nazaire on 4th February 1989, spearheading the Company's £70 million investment to challenge the Channel Tunnel across the next decade. After frustrating delays, the

The *Corbière* lays over at Cherbourg following her afternoon arrival from Poole. *(Darren Holdaway)*

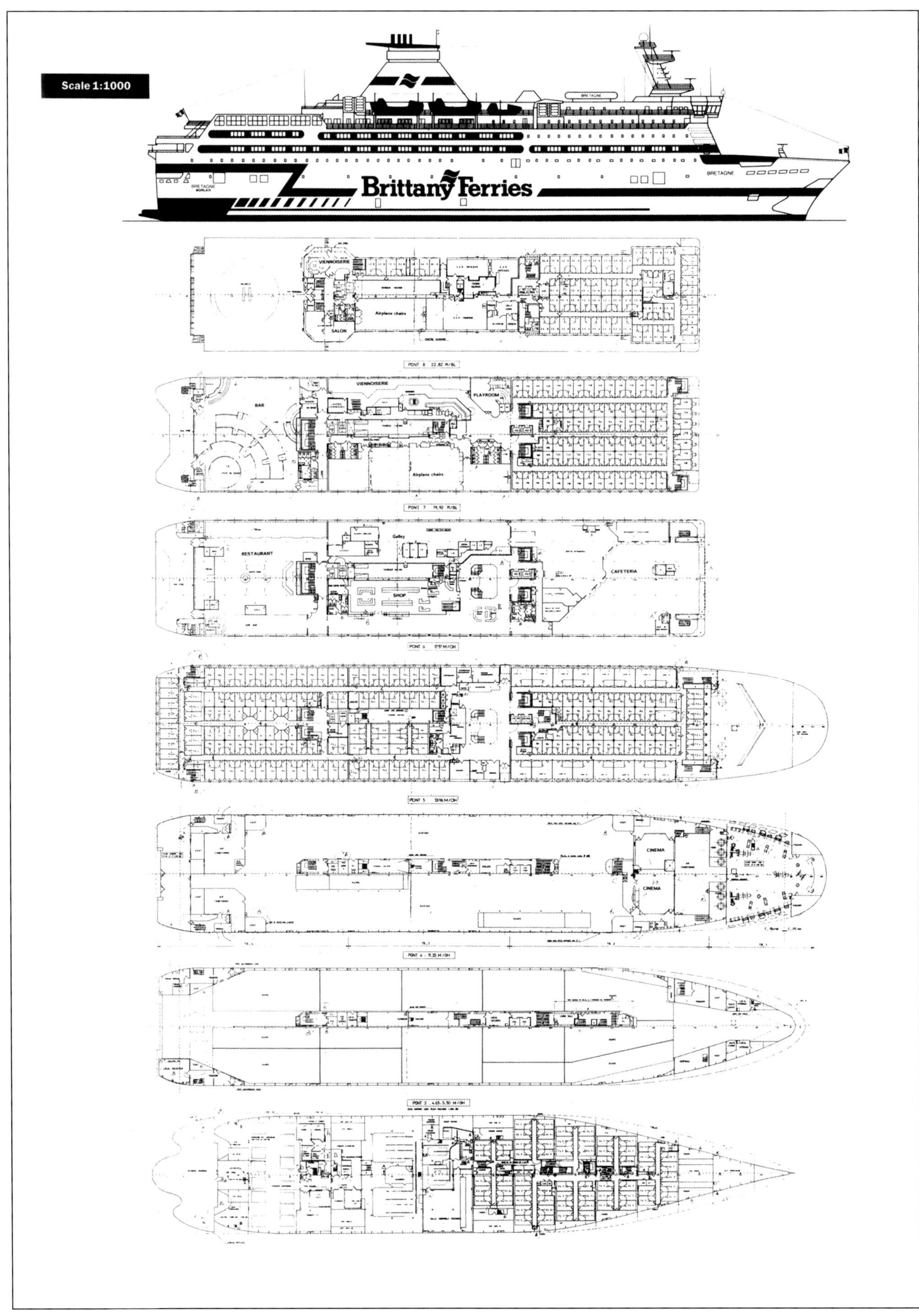
Scale 1:1000
BRETAGNE
Brittany Ferries
VIENNOISERIE
Airplane chairs
SALON
VIENNOISERIE
PLAYROOM
BAR
Airplane chairs
Galley
RESTAURANT
SHOP
CAFETERIA
CINEMA
CINEMA

Above: **Madame Bourges performs the naming of the *Bretagne*.** *(Ferry Publications Library)*

Top left: **The captain and his officers pictured on the *Bretagne*.** *(Ferry Publications Library)*

Bottom left: **The spacious main car deck of the *Bretagne*.** *(Miles Cowsill)*

Below: **Alexis Gourvennec officiates at the naming ceremony of the *Bretagne*.** *(Ferry Publications Library)*

Bretagne

Above: **The very distinctive reception area on the *Bretagne* allowed passengers to view the variety of shops on this deck, pass to their cabins or take the stairs to the upper decks.** *(Ferry Publications Library)*

Top right: **La Baule self service restaurant.** *(Ferry Publications Library)*

Below: **Le Galerie and Le Boutique on Deck 7.** *(Ferry Publications Library)*

Bottom right: **Les Abers restaurant.** *(Ferry Publications Library)*

Above: **Another view of the Les Abers restaurant.** *(Ferry Publications Library)*

Left : **Information Area.** *(Ferry Publications Library)*

Bottom left: **One of the murals by Alexander Goudie in the Les Abers restaurant.** *(Ferry Publications Library)*

Below: **A pair of Alexander Goudie's paintings that appear on the ship.** *(Ferry Publications Library)*

Bottom right: **Alexander Goudie working on the main mural destined for reception and stairwell on the *Bretagne*.** *(Lachlan Goudie collection).*

The ***Reine Mathilde*** (ex ***Prince of Brittany***) was transferred to the Caen service in 1989 to operate in tandem with the ***Duc de Normandie*** to offer extra passenger capacity on the link. *(FotoFlite)*

Fresh from her major overhaul, the ***Reine Mathilde*** arrives at Caen under the command of Captain Bertrand Apperry. *(Miles Cowsill)*

The ***Quiberon*** **was transferred to the Plymouth-Roscoff service on the entry into service of the** ***Bretagne.*** *(FotoFlite)*

new flagship belatedly slipped into Plymouth Sound on 14th July, on her delivery voyage via Roscoff. Two days later she entered commercial service. Following this, the *Quiberon* was transferred as planned, which in turn allowed the *Tregastel* to move across to the Truckline passenger service.

The *Bretagne* had an immediate impact and was soon sailing full, giving an early indication that even larger tonnage would be required in the future. The *Bretagne* experienced gearbox problems on several occasions during her maiden season and on 3rd August was forced to put into Roscoff for repair whilst on passage from Plymouth to Santander, leaving passengers with a 900-mile overland journey. Delays during the peak season were exacerbated by the tight turnarounds scheduled for each port, as her additional carrying capacity placed pressure on shore facilities, with up to 80% more business to discharge and load

The ***Bretagne*** **is escorted by two naval tugs as she enters Plymouth Sound on her first visit to the port.** *(Ferry Publications Library)*

The ***Bretagne*** **dressed overall as she enters the waterway to Cork harbour.** *(Ferry Publications Library)*

The *Quiberon* pictured fresh from her £1 million refit in 1990. *(Ferry Publications Library)*

than had previously been carried on the *Quiberon*.

The introduction of the *Bretagne* marked another landmark in the evolution of Brittany Ferries. For the first time the Company was able to match the marketing proposition of the 'Holiday Ferry' with a distinctive product that delivered the promise of a unique French on board experience. Brittany Ferries had options to build two further vessels to the *Bretagne's* design, but the pound slipped from FF11.0 to FF9.5 between spring 1989 and spring 1990, and banks were nervous about the Company's ability to manage big ships. The options lapsed.

The *Reine Mathilde* left the Portsmouth-Caen Service at the end of September 1989, leaving the *Duc de Normandie* as the sole passenger vessel on the link through the autumn and winter, with the *Trégastel* transferring from Poole to operate in a freight role, having made a very favourable impression on the Truckline service during the second half of the summer. The *Armorique* completed her season on the Portsmouth-St Malo route on 18th September and then undertook two spells of charter to support BCIF. The *Duchesse Anne* continued the service until mid-November, when she headed off for her refit, leaving the route closed for the winter. The Plymouth-Roscoff service was reduced to a largely freight-only winter operation from the end of October utilising the *Quiberon*, with the *Bretagne* operating a single weekend return passenger crossing.

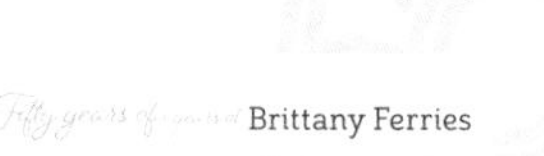

Into the 1990s

Cross-Channel ferry operators faced two significant challenges at the start of the new decade; the European Community sought to implement the withdrawal of duty-free sales concessions on internal Community transport routes from 1st January 1993, and the Channel Tunnel was scheduled to open in 1994. Both development shad the potential to severely impact revenues, and whilst there was little that could be done to prevent the latter, the industry began an intensive lobbying campaign to preserve duty-free income.

Following another record year in 1989, when some 2.1 million passengers travelled on the six-route network, Brittany Ferries sought to expand the Truckline 'Les Routiers' service to become a two-ship operation by utilising the *Corbière* running alongside the *Tregastel* for the following season. Up to four passenger departures were planned daily each way during the peak season, and with the two passenger ships and two freight vessels, the link was to see up to 16 sailings a day during 1990. Other services of the company remained unchanged for the season.

The *Quiberon* went for a £1 million refit in spring 1990. A new restaurant, larger bar, a redesigned and expanded duty-free shopping area, a new reception area, and a refurbished coffee shop and lounges were included in the work.

A small fire broke out in the engine room of the *Reine Mathilde* as she crossed from Caen to Portsmouth on 9th April. The blaze was brought under control within 40 minutes, and there was no danger to the 600 passengers on board, although the ship was in darkness for a few minutes whilst the emergency generator was started. The *Reine Mathilde* was withdrawn for repair, forcing the *Tregastel* to operate with the *Duc de Normandie* on the Portsmouth-Caen route. The

Capacity constraints frustrated traffic growth on the Poole-Cherbourg route, where the service required a multi-purpose vessel to supplement the freight ships on the route. The *Barfleur* was ordered in 1991 to support freight operations. The route's freight vessel *Purbeck* is fully loaded en route to Cherbourg. *(FotoFlite)*

An artist's impression of the forthcoming *Normandie*. *(Ferry Publications Library)*

damaged vessel remained out of service until July, which meant that the planned two-ship service on the Truckline link did not operate until the *Reine Mathilde* returned to duty. The freight vessel *Skarvøy* was later chartered to move additional summer freight.

A second high-quality vessel was needed to operate alongside the *Duc de Normandie* and consolidate the Company's growing competitive advantages on the Portsmouth-Caen route. Senacal was in robust financial health and enthusiastic to invest further in developing the fleet; investment would need to include significant enhancements in the port facilities at Portsmouth and Ouistreham to build the necessary double deck linkspans to accommodate a new vessel.

Similar capacity constraints frustrated traffic growth on the Poole-Cherbourg route, where the service required a multi-purpose vessel to supplement the freight ships on the route. A larger vessel, albeit constrained by access limitations at Poole, could deliver significant economies if it allowed the smaller, less

An artist's impression of the new Truckline vessel *Barfleur* for the Poole-Cherbourg route. *(Ferry Publications Library)*

Above: **This view shows the *Normandie* in a well-advanced stage of construction prior to the steel work for her bow section being built.** *(Ferry Publications Library)*

Top left: **The *Normandie* in the early stages of her construction.** *(Ferry Publications Library)*

Bottom left: **The bow being lifted into position.** *(Ferry Publications Library)*

Below: **The *Normandie* in her final stages of completion in the dry dock.** *(Ferry Publications Library)*

Normandie

Above: **The information area on the *Normandie* includes sculptures of famous French racehorses.** *(Ferry Publications Library)*

Top right: **The outside area of Le Deauville restaurant.** *(Ferry Publications Library)*

Bottom right: **A two-berth luxury cabin on Deck 7.** *(Ferry Publications Library)*

Below: **The attractive bar area on board the *Normandie* located on deck 8.** *(Ferry Publications Library)*

efficient ships to be withdrawn. Port facilities at Poole and Cherbourg would also require significant investment. The outcome was the establishment in Saint-Lô in April 1991 of a third SEM, the Société d'Équipement Naval de la Manche (Senamanche), with a shareholding split between the Basse Normandie region, the Calvados département, and Brittany Ferries. This used the same funding approach as Sabemen and Senacal. Operating in a similar way to the two sister SEMs, Senamanche would provide the funding for fleet investment on the route.

With financial backing in place, discussions continued with shipyards for what was now a potential two-ship order based on the involvement of two SEMs. This time no French shipyards were able to deliver the order to the required tight timescales and price. Brittany Ferries announced an order for two vessels on 17th May. The contract for the first vessel, later to be named the *Normandie*, was signed in May with the Masa shipyard of Turku, Finland. The 27,000-gt *Normandie*, destined for the Portsmouth-Caen route, would bring capacity for 2,120 passengers and 600 cars. The contract price was FF769.6 million, supported by public aid of FF40.0 million.

The original plan was for a second sister vessel, but the Masa shipyard was committed to other projects, so a smaller design was developed, more appropriate for the physical constraints of Poole harbour. Masa had a suitable building slot available at their Helsinki shipyard. The construction contract for the *Barfleur* (named after the Cotentin harbour village) of FF495.1 million, supported by public aid of FF40.0 million, was signed by Senamanche with the Masa Helsinki shipyard on 20th September, with construction planned to start in March 1991. The 18,000-gt *Barfleur* would bring capacity for 1,200 passengers and carry 270 cars and 70 freight vehicles, or 118 freight vehicles on freight-only sailings. She was designed to fit the constraints of Poole Harbour's narrow approach channel, as even with a 5.8 metre draught there would be only two metres of water under her hull at low tide.

In July the newly formed Sealink Stena Line announced their intention to inaugurate a new Southampton-Cherbourg service from the 1991 season, utilising the 1982-built *St Nicholas* from their Harwich-Hoek of Holland route. The 149.0-metre-long and 28.0 metre beam vessel had capacity for 2,200 passengers and 700 cars and would be renamed *Stena Normandy* for the Southampton service.

The *Armorique* damaged a propeller whilst docking at St Malo on 6th September, leaving her with one serviceable engine for the remainder of her season until 1st October, pending a complete repair. Her St Malo schedule quickly proved unsustainable, so she was confined to operate between Portsmouth and Cherbourg with a lengthy six- to seven-hour passage time. Passengers faced a long drive through the Cotentin peninsula.

The *Armorique* dressed overall for the arrival of the *Normandie* at Ouistreham with the *Normandie Shipper* in the background. *(Ferry Publications Library)*

The *Coutances* was chartered to the French government from 23rd September to help convey troops to support the Gulf War, sailing via the Suez Canal to Yanbu, Saudi Arabia. The *Havelet* was transferred from BCIF to Truckline to replace her, and the *Corbière* switched to BCIF until the *Coutances* returned. The *Armorique* was also chartered by the French government on 27th December for similar work following her repair.

1990 was another successful year, with further growth in passenger traffic and a recovery in the freight sector. Passenger carryings reached 2,638,847, a rise of 24.6%, vehicle traffic rose by 19.1% to hit 627,887 and freight volumes saw 3.0% growth to reach 151,452. Turnover reached FF1.7 billion. The Poole-Cherbourg service experienced a 98% rise in passenger traffic, despite all the issues with the transfer of the *Trégastel* away from the route during the early season.

The combined capital of the three SEMs Sabemen, Senacal and Senamanche, increased to FF 375 million at the start of 1991 to finance the building of the *Normandie* and the *Barfleur* on top of the existing investment in the *Bretagne*. This was deemed essential to accommodate the growth in traffic being experienced by Brittany Ferries.

Long standing rumours were confirmed in July 1991 when it became clear that P&O European Ferries were in discussion with Vapores Suardíaz about a joint venture to operate a twice-weekly ferry service from Portsmouth to Bilbao. This news accelerated the Company's plans to find a replacement for the *Bretagne*, which was now operating at capacity on the Plymouth-Santander route.

The *Barfleur* was floated out in Helsinki on 27/28th July, with the *Normandie* following in Turku on 5th October. As the *Barfleur* underwent sea trials it became evident that she was suffering from severe deadweight problems. Fortunately, her design had incorporated the future ability to stretch the vessel by inserting up to three nine-metre sections to provide additional capacity; adding one section solved the deadweight problem,

Captain Bertrand Apperry with Madame Garrec, Godmother of the ***Normandie***, and Father Olivier Pellen, pictured in Rotterdam at the blessing of the vessel. *(Ferry Publications Library)*

A superb study of the graceful lines of the ***Normandie*** as she arrives at Ouistreham for the first time following her blessing at Rotterdam. The ***Normandie Shipper*** is pictured at the original berth at the port. *(Ferry Publications Library)*

The ***Normandie*** **is passed by the** ***Duc de Normandie*** **whilst at Portsmouth on her debut to the British press, prior to entering service.** *(Miles Cowsill)*

increasing her length by nine metres to 157 metres, but delaying her entry into service. The additional work began on 22nd December and the work was undertaken at cost by the shipyard.

With the imminent arrival of two new vessels, steps were taken to dispose of surplus vessels. The *Corbière* made her final crossing from Cherbourg to Poole on 22nd September 1991 and was sold to Oy Eckerölinjens A.B. The *Trégastel* completed her scheduled duties on the Poole-Cherbourg route on 29th September, with the *Reine Mathilde* finishing the following day. The *Trégastel* operated in freight-only mode on the Portsmouth-Caen service prior to being handed over to P&O Scottish Ferries early in 1992, to operate as the *St Clair* on services from Aberdeen to Lerwick. The *Reine Mathilde* was sold to the Nassau-based company Marine Invest in 1991; she was soon chartered back to BCIF to replace the *Rozel* as the renamed *Beauport* for 1992/3.

Brittany Ferries could reflect on a business that grew

Part of the forward cafeteria area on the ***Barfleur.*** *(Ferry Publications Library)*

The self-service restaurant on the ***Barfleur.*** *(Ferry Publications Library)*

by 2.8% in 1991 to reach 2,712,000 passengers. Cross-Channel traffic accounted for 2,490,000 of this, with the remainder travelling to Santander and Cork. Vehicle traffic continued to make more spectacular progress, rising by 14.8% to reach 720,799 vehicles, whilst freight traffic crept upwards by 2.3% to record 154,899 units. This performance resulted in a net profit of FF41.6 million compared to FF32.2 million in 1989-90, a rise of 29.2%, with turnover increasing to FF1.83 billion from FF1.69 billion (up 8.3%). Passenger and vehicle income grew by 12.7% to reach FF1.26 billion, freight revenue totalled FF 357 million, whilst the holiday business income grew by 7.6% to FF170 million.

In the 1991 season the number of bed-nights booked through Brittany Ferries Holidays hit one million for the first time, with more than 20% of passengers booking an inclusive holiday or tour, and business more than tripling through the preceding decade.

With new capacity coming for the Poole-Cherbourg and Portsmouth-Caen routes, attention turned to how the increasing levels of traffic on the Portsmouth-St Malo and Plymouth-Santander routes could be accommodated in the future. Traffic volumes on the Plymouth-Santander route were stretching the capabilities of the *Bretagne*, but if she was replaced by a larger-capacity vessel to Spain she would make an excellent ship for the Portsmouth-St Malo service. In early 1992 the partners in Sabemen (now owners of the *Armorique, Bretagne, Duchesse Anne*, and *Quiberon*) voted to double their capital investment in the SEM with a view to acquiring a new vessel in 1993 and take advantage of the port improvements being planned to accommodate larger vessels in St Malo.

The *Duc de Normandie* received an extensive £3 million refit in January 1992, including an upgrade to her passenger accommodation so that her facilities were of a high standard prior to the *Normandie* entering service. The *Armorique* and *Quiberon* covered the Caen service until the refurbished 'Duc' returned in March, with the *Armorique* remaining in a support role until the arrival of the *Normandie*. Work also started in Portsmouth and Ouistreham on building new double-decker linkspans and berth extensions for the new 27,000-gt flagship; the work at Ouistreham was supplemented by dredging to enable the *Normandie* to use the port in all weathers. Similar works were required at Poole, with £26 million spent to prepare for the introduction of the two new vessels. Staying ahead of competitors, a new £10 million computer reservation system was introduced, reflecting the complexity of the booking process and the holiday business.

The decision to stretch the *Barfleur* forced her to miss the planned January introduction to the Poole-Cherbourg route. The *Normandie Shipper* covered the service whilst the *Purbeck* was transferred to cover refits on the Portsmouth-Caen route. The *Duchesse Anne* helped on the freight service in January, and re-opened

the St Malo service from 1st to 21st March, operating to Poole because of the ongoing linkspan construction works at Portsmouth; the *Armorique* joined her from 20th May. The *Quiberon* left the Roscoff service on 17th March to take up the Caen roster, with the *Duc de Normandie* replacing her.

The *Barfleur*, resplendent in her yellow and grey Truckline livery, successfully completed her second sea trials in early March, and arrived in Poole for the first time on 4th April ready for the opening ceremony for the new double deck linkspan on Berth 3, unveiled by Alexis Gourvennec. The eight-deck ship, now with capacity for 1,304 passengers and 600 cars or a combination of 304 cars and 66 freight vehicles, offered new standards for the four-hour link. Prince Edward inspected and lunched on board the *Barfleur* in Poole on 7th April. She made a freight-only crossing to Cherbourg on 14th April, followed by her maiden passenger sailing the next day. The schedule required the *Barfleur* to undertake two round trips daily through the summer season, replacing three ships on the route, and she soon came under capacity pressure at peak periods. Thus, a second ship would be needed for the 1993 season if the route's potential was not to be left frustrated.

Meanwhile, the *Normandie* was nearing completion at the Masa-Turku shipyard in Finland. She had been launched on 5th October 1991 and undertook successful sea trials off Finland in wintry conditions during March 1992; she was handed over to Brittany Ferries at the shipyard on 5th May. She then sailed to Beatrixhaven, Holland for her naming ceremony; industrial action prevented this taking place in Caen as planned. The *Normandie* then sailed to Ouistreham and Portsmouth for berthing trials, returning to Ouistreham on her inaugural 08:00 sailing on 18th May, replacing the *Reine Mathilde*, and instantly providing a 40% increase in capacity on the route. The new vessel boasted 220 luxury cabins and capacity for 2,120 passengers with space for 630 cars on two decks. The interior of the 10-deck *Normandie* and its range of on-board facilities had been created specifically to offer guests a level of comfort, style and space normally associated with cruise

The **Barfleur**, dressed overall, arriving at the entrance to Poole harbour on her maiden voyage to the Dorset port. *(Miles Cowsill)*

The **Barfleur** sporting the Truckline livery for the route. From 1999 she was repainted in full Brittany Ferries colours. *(Ferry Publications Library)*

Normandie *(FotoFlite)*

ANDIE

The *Duc de Normandie* passes her running partner on the Caen service shortly after the introduction of the *Normandie*. *(FotoFlite)*

ships. Aboard the new flagship were two cinema lounges, the duty-free shopping mall, a choice of restaurants and bars, children's video and entertainment area, playroom for the very young and a fully equipped hospital. All cabins were air conditioned with private shower and toilet facilities and lounges were equipped with reclining seats akin to those found in business class sections of long-haul airlines.

With the introduction of the *Barfleur* and now the *Normandie*, the average age of the Brittany Ferries fleet was just 9.4 years, making it the youngest of any ferry operator on the English Channel. This reflected the fact the Company had made significantly greater capital investment than any other cross-channel operator to meet the impending challenge of the Channel Tunnel.

Fire broke out in the *Quiberon's* main engine room on 17th July after the vessel had left Plymouth for Roscoff with 1,124 passengers, 94 crew and 243 cars on board. She was 60 miles off the French coast when the fire began just after 11:15. The blaze was extinguished within an hour, but damage was sufficient to send the *Quiberon* to Brest for repairs after discharging her passengers and vehicles in Roscoff. Passengers praised the captain and his crew for their handling of the emergency, the cause of which was believed to be a ruptured pipe. Sadly, Alain Etienne, a 28-year-old French crewman, died after being asphyxiated by fumes whilst trying to put out the fire.

The incident resulted in the immediate halving of the Plymouth-Roscoff schedule at the peak of the season, forcing traffic to transfer to the Cherbourg and Caen routes. The *Armorique* switched from Portsmouth-St Malo to Poole-Cherbourg to offer an enhanced frequency on the route, and the *Coutances* also switched from Plymouth to Poole to supplement the *Purbeck's* freight capacity. The cost of repairing the *Quiberon* was high, and her insurers considered writing her off at one stage, but eventually authorised the remedial work. Sailings did not return to normal until the *Quiberon* resumed on 28th August

On 9th December 1992 the *Duchesse Anne* was in collision with the French dredger *Le Timac* as she approached St Malo from Portsmouth. The *Duchesse Anne* went to Brest for repair, with the *Armorique* brought in to cover her absence. The *Armorique* made her final sailing for Brittany Ferries on 30th December with the 21:30 from Portsmouth to St Malo and was de-stored and laid up at Bassin Vauban in St Malo, prior to being put up for sale.

1992 was a difficult year for all operators on the western Channel. Group turnover rose to FF1,342 million and the Company made a net profit of FF22.1 million. Brittany Ferries saw passenger volumes fall by 2.7% to 2,639,803 and there was a small drop in vehicle traffic of 1.3% to 711,291 cars. Freight traffic continued to rise, with a further 8.7% increase in units carried.

Enter the Val de Loire

The search for a vessel with sufficient capacity to improve on the *Bretagne* yet be capable of handling sea conditions in the Bay of Biscay focused on the 1987-built TT-Line vessel *Nils Holgersson*. She was inspected in early January 1993 and her £40 million purchase to support the Roscoff, Cork and Santander routes was announced publicly on 2nd February. The *Nils Holgersson* offered a modest increase in passenger capacity over the *Bretagne* but incorporated many more cabins and a bigger car deck. The 31,360-gt vessel was 161.5 metres in length and could carry 2,280 passengers and 570 cars.

The *Nils Holgersson* underwent a short overhaul at the Flender Werft shipyard at Lübeck in Germany, before emerging as the *Val de Loire* and heading to the Ankommer INMA shipyard in La Spezia, Italy, for more extensive works, that included the reconstruction and reinforcing of her bow. The £70 million refurbishment cost brought the acquisition cost of the *Val de Loire* to some £120 million. Consideration was given to acquiring the *Val de Loire's* two sisters to enable a complete fleet renewal, but the additional need for appropriate refurbishment made this too expensive a proposition. The two vessels were eventually to appear in the Western Channel in competition to Brittany Ferries.

The *Val de Loire* was re-equipped with new Commodore Class Cabins and a dedicated lounge on Deck 10; the main passenger facilities were located on Decks 7 (the Panoramic Lounge, duty-free shop and self-service restaurant 'La Magdalena'), 8 (the à la carte restaurant 'Le Temps de Vivre', the bistro 'Le Café du Port', the tea shop 'Le Grand Large', and the piano bar 'Le Layon'), and 9 (the beauty centre, a photo shop and the bar 'Le Relais'). On Deck 1 could be found a Swimming Pool – a first for a cruise ferry - a Night Club, two Cinemas, and a Children Playroom.

The *Val de Loire* was given a maritime theme throughout the vessel, making liberal use of detailed models of 20th century Atlantic Ocean liners, with items of appropriate memorabilia, including sextants, searchlights, compasses, and telescopes. More original artwork by Alexander Goudie and other artists enhanced the vessel. The 'Le Temps de Vivre' restaurant was decorated with watercolour paintings of the Loire Valley to help create a calming atmosphere, whilst 'Le Cafe du Port' and 'Le Grand Large' used images of fishing from Roscoff, with special stained-glass murals. The Commodore Class cabins were each named after different wines from the Loire Valley, with an appropriate complimentary bottle offered to occupants on Spanish sailings.

The *Nils Holgersson* prior to her sale to Brittany Ferries. *(Ferry Publications Library)*

An early artist's impression of the *Val de Loire* following the Company's acquisition of the vessel. *Ferry Publications Library)*

The abolition of duty-free sales for journeys made entirely within the EU was originally agreed by the European Commission in 1991, on the grounds that cut-price sales to cross-border travellers was an anomaly within a single market. The date for abolition was set as 1st January 1993 to coincide with the start of the new single market. As the deadline loomed, the duty-free sector successfully lobbied for a reversal of the decision, and the ferry industry (and other transport operations) was granted an extra six and a half years to adjust their trading arrangements and prepare for the loss of

Top: **The *Val de Loire* was purchased from the German ferry company TT-Line in 1992 and went to Italy for a major overhaul and rebuilding of her bow door section to improve her sea-riding qualities for the Bay of Biscay.** *(Ian Carruthers collection)*

Above: **The *Val de Loire* pictured from the Plymouth pilot boat as she heads out of the port for Santander.** *(Miles Cowsill)*

'Le Temps de Vivre' restaurant on the ***Val de Loire.*** *(Miles Cowsill)*

revenue. The new abolition date became 30th June 1999.

The *Bretagne* opened the Portsmouth-Santander winter service on 28th January, then transferred to Plymouth to cover the Roscoff/Cork/Santander rotation from 17th March until the arrival of the *Val de Loire* on 16th June. The lack of any passenger service on the Plymouth-Roscoff route during the winter was not well received and there were strong local protests.

Meanwhile, P&O European Ferries secured the charter of the 1986-built cruise ferry *Olympia* from Viking Line to open their new service to Bilbao. She could carry 2,500 passengers and 580 cars, with cabin accommodation for all passengers. She sailed from the Baltic on 6th April for a short overhaul in Southampton, prior to emerging as the *Pride of Bilbao* in time for her inaugural voyage from Portsmouth to Bilbao on 28th April. Her weekly schedule encompassed two round trips to Spain and a weekend crossing from Portsmouth to Cherbourg, providing valuable extra capacity on the French route.

In the first annual survey of ferries, Brittany Ferries was awarded five-star ratings by the AA for the excellent standards of service and facilities on both the *Normandie* and *Bretagne*, making it the only company on the English Channel to receive this highest accolade. The Company won praise for the quality of on-board self-service restaurants, winning four out of the six category awards; the *Barfleur's* Turquoise Restaurant was voted the outright winner for maintaining high standards and offering a good display of hot and cold food and freshly baked pastries in a bright and welcoming décor.

The *Val de Loire* left La Spezia in late May and sailed to Santander ready for berthing trials in the port on 2nd

Le Grande Large - Tea Shop on the ***Val de Loire.*** *(Miles Cowsill)*

The ***Val de Loire*** Reception and information area. *(Miles Cowsill)*

Val de Loire *(Miles Cowsill)*

June. Following receptions in Plymouth and Roscoff, the *Val de Loire* entered service between Plymouth and Santander on 7th June, making her first visit to Cork from Roscoff on 12th June. Her arrival allowed the *Bretagne* to transfer to the Portsmouth-St Malo route, as planned, from 14th June. The displaced *Duchesse Anne* then switched to cover the Plymouth-Roscoff service alongside the *Quiberon*, to help deliver a timetable of up to three daily departures on the route; the *Duchesse Anne* also covered the Roscoff-Cork route and opened a new seasonal weekly Cork-St Malo service from 21st June.

The *Purbeck* was withdrawn in the autumn and laid up prior to a potential sale to the holding company Channel Island Ferries, whilst the *Coutances* remained on the Poole-Cherbourg route to operate alongside the *Barfleur*. The redundant *Armorique* was sold to the Chinese Government in early December for further operations in the Far East, sailing between Xiamen and Hong Kong as the *Min Nan*. She left St Malo for the last time on 18th December, bound for China.

Brittany Ferries reported a loss of FF12.3 million in 1993 on a turnover of FF1.389.6 million, despite passenger carryings increasing by 5.8% to 2.79 million, vehicle traffic by 4.8% to 74,551 and commercial vehicles by 4.8% to 177,023 during the year. Income was hit by deteriorating exchange rates, with the pound languishing around FF8.5 for much of the year; there was to be a further gradual slide of the currency for the next two years. This highlighted the problems for a Company for whom most of the income was in one currency, with much of the expenditure in another.

The winter sun catches the *Val De Loire* as she arrives at Portsmouth from Santander. *(Miles Cowsill)*

The *Armorique* lies next to the town walls of St Malo during one of her winter lay-ups. *(Miles Cowsill)*

The *Val de Loire* and *Bretagne* pass each other in Plymouth Sound prior to the former German ship entering service. *(Ferry Publications Library)*

Restructuring to survive

Brittany Ferries celebrated its 21st birthday at the start of 1994 having achieved a market share of more than 50% on the western Channel and built a business that was now carrying almost three million passengers each year. The Company had the youngest fleet on the English Channel, the largest ship (the *Normandie*), and boasted the completion of a £350 million fleet investment programme that included the acquisition of the *Barfleur, Normandie* and *Val de Loire*. More routes were operated on the English Channel than by any other operator, with a further two services between Ireland and France. The fleet sailed the equivalent of 35 circumnavigations of the globe each year. Each summer, the Company served three million meals and operated hotels with a nightly capacity for 6,200 guests; five and a half times the combined bed space of the Dorchester, the Savoy, and Claridge's, in London. Serestel was having a major impact on the quality of on-board services, and ship's pursers were now predominantly professionals recruited directly from the hotel sector to bring the 'floating hotel' concept to life. Over 1,000 passenger-facing staff, from pursers to musicians, were employed across the fleet, and Brittany Ferries was the only ferry company to employ a doctor an all its ships. Duty free sales were equivalent to a large supermarket, with 100 million cigarettes and 260,000 bottles of perfume sold each year. And the Company was the leading tour operator of motoring holidays to France and Spain, in a business with a £20 million annual turnover.

The end of Brittany Ferries involvement in the operation of Channel Island services was announced on 7th January 1994 and implemented on the 23rd of that month. The Brittany Ferries shareholding interest remained in Channel Island Ferries as a ship-owning company, managed from the UK operation; the *Purbeck* was retained on charter by Commodore, whilst the *Havelet* remained on charter to Condor, both with the owner's deck and engine crew.

Brittany Ferries' ninth route was launched on 14th

The *Quiberon* arrives at Ringaskiddy (Cork) on her overnight sailing from Roscoff. *(Miles Cowsill)*

Armorique *(FotoFlite)*

May when the *Duchesse Anne* opened the Poole-St Malo link with an eight-hour crossing time, offering four round trips each week around her sailings from St Malo to Cork. She operated outwards by day from Poole and returned overnight, dovetailing into the established service from Portsmouth and complementing the links to Cherbourg from the port.

The most challenging event of 1994 was the formal opening of the Channel Tunnel on 6th May. The first revenue-earning train ran through the Tunnel on 19th May, almost a year behind schedule. The impact was almost immediate as a ferocious price war ensued with fares falling as low as £30 for a return crossing for a car and passengers on the short sea routes. Eurotunnel's sought to cause widespread disruption to the ferry industry, by wiping out as many routes as possible, and changing the dynamics of cross-Channel travel. The situation was not helped when Brittany Ferries faced further blockades in the French ports, as French and Spanish fishermen engaged in another 'tuna war'.

P&O European Ferries had been searching for replacements for their 'Super Viking' fleet on the Le Havre route for some time, but their requirement for two identical vessels proved difficult. They were becoming increasingly desperate as they fell behind the fleet investment made by Brittany Ferries. Sisters of the *Val de Loire*, the *Olau Britannia* and *Olau Hollandia* were employed on the Sheerness-Vlissingen service, but Olau Line closed the route from May 1994, citing the Channel Tunnel and union resistance to cost-saving proposals. Of 33,336 gross tonnage, 161 metres in length, the sisters carried 1,716 passengers, all of whom could be accommodated in cabin berths, 575 cars or 118 trailers, at a top speed of 21.3 knots. P&O European Ferries secured the vessels under a five-year charter arrangement, and they entered service in early summer.

The *Val de Loire* joined the *Normandie* on the Portsmouth-Caen route from the late summer, with the *Bretagne* deployed to cover the winter Portsmouth-Santander and Portsmouth-St Malo routes.

The year ended on a mixed note. Despite all the price pressure from further east in the Channel, Brittany Ferries recorded a 5.8% increase in carryings across all routes, but the further fall in the value of sterling against the French Franc pushed the Company deeper into trading loss. Passenger carryings broke through the three million level for the first and only time in the Company's history, reaching 3,022,198. Vehicle carryings also hit a record 738,194 cars, and freight volumes hit another record 192,451 units, a figure that was not to be surpassed until 2004.

In January 1995, 'The Times' forecast that 1995 and 1996 would be the bloodiest years ever seen for ferry operators on the English Channel, predicting that either P&O European Ferries or Stena Line would be forced to reduce frequencies in the face of full operation of

Eurotunnel's 'Le Shuttle' services.

In early 1995 Brittany Ferries opened talks with the port of Bayonne in southwest France on a new service from the UK to the French port but did not progress the idea as analysis suggested that the route could have a detrimental effect on carryings of the Santander route.

The *Bretagne* was joined by the *Duc de Normandie* for the winter Portsmouth-St Malo service, with the latter providing a St Malo-Plymouth positioning trip to enable the Company to offer weekend sailings from Plymouth to Roscoff, thereby providing a year-round service again. The *Val de Loire* re-opened the Plymouth-Santander service on 17th March

The Portsmouth-St Malo services saw record carryings during the summer of 1995, prompting the expansion of the winter service to five round trips each week with the *Duc de Normandie* and *Bretagne*. The *Duc de Normandie* replaced the *Quiberon* on the Plymouth-Roscoff service at weekends and operated a balancing St Malo-Plymouth sailing on Fridays and Mondays. The *Val de Loire* remained with the *Normandie* on the Portsmouth-Caen service through the winter, with the *Bretagne* covering Spain. Both the *Quiberon* and *Duchesse Anne* were laid up for the winter.

1995 was another difficult year. Sterling fell to a rate of FF7.7 in the second quarter of the year, recovering to FF7.9 by the year end. The sustained devaluation of sterling brought the equivalent of a FF120 million drop in revenue, and social tax differentials paid to French employees led to an additional estimated FF40 million charges. The opening of the Channel Tunnel continued to hit financial performance hard. It was the almost perfect storm. Net losses in the year ending September 1995 reached FF80.3 million, as group turnover fell by over eleven per cent to FF1,285 million. Passenger numbers were down by four per cent to 2,779,418. Over 50,000 fewer cars were carried as the volume fell to 681,734, whilst freight traffic slipped to 185,807 units.

After strong lobbying of the French government, the social tax burden was resolved in in mid-March 1996 with the award of a FF40 million grant to cover crew

Built at Verolme Cork Dockyards Ltd in Cork, the former B&I Line ferry ***Connacht*** is seen here as the ***Duchesse Anne*** at Ringaskiddy following her arrival from St Malo. *(Miles Cowsill)*

Crowds watch from the bow as the ***Bretagne*** arrives at Portsmouth. *(Miles Cowsill)*

The ***Val de Loire*** leaves Santander for Plymouth. The ferries arriving from Plymouth and Portsmouth were a regular sight for beachcombers and walkers twice-weekly during the late eighties and nineties; today there are up to seven sailings a week coming into Santander. *(Miles Cowsill)*

The ***Normandie Shipper*** (ex ***Speedlink Vanguard***) and ***Barfleur*** pass each other in the English Channel. The former train ferry remained on charter to Truckline for just under six years. *(FotoFlite)*

social costs; this enabled Brittany Ferries to match the similar charges paid by their British flag competitors. Further relief came when the shareholders of each SEM (excluding Brittany Ferries) agreed to increase their capital holding in each SEM, to enable a three-year waiver of vessel rents accompanied by a 'better fortunes' mechanism to recover this sum as trading conditions improved; Brittany Ferries' proportion of the shares in each SEM was reduced accordingly. Once again, the French funding structure demonstrated its ability to provide support to sustain a socially important business.

The reduction in short-term costs was accompanied by a business review that prompted the financial restructuring measures necessary to make substantial organisation changes, whilst implementing a fleet renewal strategy to acquire a new vessel, then codenamed *Normandie 2*, to replace the ageing *Quiberon*. The new three-year plan envisaged a route to return to profitability, although the ability to sustain this performance in the longer-term was deemed uncertain, as fluctuations in exchange rates, competitor strategies and the impact of the future loss of duty-free revenues were each likely to have a further uncontrollable impact on the business. The French government also offered two tranches of financial support valued at FF70 million and FF80 million. But the Plan required Brittany Ferries to make economies by closing the routes to St Malo from Poole and Cork at the end of the 1996 season and place the *Normandie Shipper* and *Coutances* up for sale.

The *Quiberon* was sold to the Trovil Shipping Company and leased back, with rental payments spread over the period from 1995 to 2001. Meanwhile, the financing period for the *Val de Loire* was extended by a further three years, with the additional interest costs passed through Sabemen to Brittany Ferries. These two actions relieved financial pressure on the SEMs but further helped to stabilise the Company's finances. The cumulative effect of all these measures under the three-year Plan was to generate financial savings of FF60 million in 1996 and FF50 million in 1997, with the intention of reducing the deficit by 60% in 1997 and eliminating it altogether in 1998.

The service pattern was unchanged for the 1996 season, with fares restructured to match those on the short-sea cross-Channel routes to meet the continuing price challenge from the Channel Tunnel.

The *Duchesse Anne* made her final sailing with Brittany Ferries on 30th September 1996 and was withdrawn for sale. She was purchased by Jadrolinija P.O. of Rijeka, Croatia the following month, and renamed the *Dubrovnik*.

The 1996 season ended with a further downturn in business from the peaks of 1994. Passenger carryings dropped to 2,497,105, a fall of nine per cent year on year and almost 18% over two years. Vehicles numbers fell to 593,705, down 13%, and freight by 9% to 168,581 units. Brittany Ferries made a trading loss of FF16.21 million in the financial year, a significant improvement on the FF80.26 million loss made in 1995.

The *Stena Normandy* made her last crossing for Stena Line on the Southampton-Cherbourg route on 30th November and was de-stored at Southampton prior to being withdrawn and sent to Falmouth for lay-up.

Meanwhile, Brittany Ferries and P&O European Ferries entered talks to consider a possible merger of their respective operations on the Western Channel. There were many synergies between the two companies and significant opportunities for consolidation and rationalisation of services, but in the event the companies decided not to join forces. The winter service of Brittany Ferries for 1996 was to see a similar pattern to that of the previous year with the *Val de Loire* operating in tandem with the *Normandie* on Portsmouth-Caen whilst the *Bretagne* maintained the Santander and St Malo operations.

With the rescue plan ratified and a clear path to financial recovery in place, it was an appropriate time for Christian Michielini to retire after more than 20 years leading the Company. This was the end of an era. His tenure was marked by the successful professionalisation of the business following the difficulties of the early years, followed by a sustained period of route expansion, fleet acquisition and modernisation. On board services had been transformed to become widely recognised as market-leading in both quality and service. Branding was clear, consistent, and instantly recognisable. The fleet now comprised of the youngest average of vessels of any ferry company operating on the English Channel. Financial stability had been enhanced by the incorporation of the SEMs and their funding model at the heart of the business. And the Company held the predominant share of business on the western Channel. He left a secure and stable company on the way to recovery, after the most bruising price war ever witnessed in the cross-Channel market.

Christian Michielini left the Company on 30th April 1997; his ambitions to retire to buy land and breed horses were not fully realised and his planned years of retirement were prematurely cut short. He was replaced as General Manager by 47-year-old Claude Geronimi, brought into the Company from Elf Oil.

The summer 1997 season proved to be very busy as sterling recovered to 10FF. This was reflected in the financial results, with a healthy increase in turnover, profits, and carryings. Turnover rose by 14.5% to reach FF1,694 million, with profit after tax reaching FF84.5 million. Market share of the western channel passenger traffic rose to 49%, with car traffic reaching 53%, and freight carryings achieved a 49% share. Passenger carryings reached 2,635,119; 722,813 cars and 186,205 freight vehicles were carried. This was a fitting epitaph for Christian Michielini.

The *Barfleur* was deployed on the weekend Santander service for the 1997/8 winter programme in place of the *Bretagne*, operating from Poole on a 28-hour passage to test the freight market. The movement of lorries on French roads was restricted at weekends and the Barfleur offered a by-pass to the controls. Her passenger certificate was reduced to 200 passengers whilst operating this service. The *Barfleur* ran her normal service between Poole and Cherbourg for the rest of the week. Meanwhile, the Portsmouth-St Malo route had an enhanced winter weekend service featuring a combination of the *Quiberon* and the *Bretagne*.

Surprisingly, General Manager Claude Geronimi left the Company in December 1997, after less than nine months in the role. It was still felt that it would be appropriate for another 'outsider' to run the Company on a day-to-day basis and his replacement was 49-year-old Jean-Michel Masson, who joined the Company from the Air France group.

On 26th March 1998 P&O Portsmouth announced the charter of the fast craft *Superstar Express* from Star Cruises to supplement existing services on the Portsmouth-Cherbourg route from mid-May until September

Brittany Ferries attracted good levels of business during the summer season especially on the Portsmouth-St Malo service, which encouraged the repeated deployment of the *Bretagne* and *Quiberon* on the route; the *Quiberon* was deployed at weekends on the St Malo-Plymouth-Roscoff service to supplement services in the west. The *Val de Loire* returned to Portsmouth on 16th November to maintain the Caen service over the winter with the *Normandie*. Meanwhile the *Barfleur* was again employed on the winter Poole-Cherbourg and Poole-Santander routes. The Spanish service was suspended from 3rd January until 5th February during the period of the *Barfleur* refit.

The first steps of the recovery plan were beginning to have an impact. The company reported an increase of 10.7% in turnover to FF1,875 million, generating a pre-tax profit of FF134.4 million. Prudently this profit was reduced to FF10.2 million after tax provision for repayment of the French government support grant, which was still subject to European Commission approval. Masson noted that FF250 million (€38.11 million) of vessel rent had been postponed under the recovery plan, but repayment would begin in 1999. The Company was able to record a 49.5% share of passenger movements and 50% share of freight traffic across the western Channel routes. Brittany Ferries had carried 2,656,900 passengers (up 0.4%), 736,610 cars (up 6%) and 180, 630 freight units.

All Brittany Ferries routes were brought under a single corporate branding for the 1999 season. The independence of the Truckline brand had served its purpose, particularly in the early days of the Les Routiers passenger service and as a distinguishing brand for all freight operations, but standards on the *Barfleur* were consistent with those across the rest of the fleet, and more efficiencies could be achieved through one clear brand identity. The *Barfleur* was repainted in the full Brittany Ferries livery.

New Year's Day 1999 saw the launch of the 'Euro' across Europe, marking the end for the French Franc. This could have solved a significant issue if income and expenditure were now in the same currency but Britain's insistence on sterling remaining outside the common currency perpetuated Brittany Ferries' problems. The EU also stood ready to finally implement the ending of duty-free sales in July 1999 which placed further pressure on operating profits. However, Brittany Ferries was much less dependent on this income than many of its competitors, who's notorious 'booze-cruises' and newspaper offers were significant sources of revenue.

The *Normandie Shipper* was sold in October 1999 to Adecon Shipping of the Bahamas, as part of the three-year restructuring plan; she was registered to Bonavista Shipping Corporation and renamed the *Bonavista*.

The winter operating pattern was repeated, with the *Val de Loire* returning to the Portsmouth-Caen route alongside the *Normandie*, and the *Barfleur* covering during their refits with the *Duc de Normandie* maintaining the Poole-Cherbourg service during the *Barfleur's* absence. The *Quiberon* worked the weekend Plymouth-Roscoff service, undertaking its usual Plymouth-St Malo repositioning trip, and supporting the *Bretagne* on the Portsmouth-St Malo route during the week. The Spanish service was suspended from 16th November 1999 until mid-March 2000.

Brittany Ferries reported a further year of improved financial results in 1998-9, with turnover increasing by 4.1% to £195 million, despite the loss of duty-free revenues during the summer. The company recorded a profit of £17.2 million, an increase of 27% on the previous year. Brittany Ferries carried 2,654,165 passengers, 762,650 cars and 172,950 freight vehicles giving a 52.2% share of western Channel passengers (from 49.5%) and 53.7% of freight (from 50%). Over the three financial years that followed the restructuring plan, the Company had, as planned, fully reimbursed the reduced charter payments agreed with their shipowner partners in 1996. This gave the SEMs the confidence to consider investment in another new vessel.

Brittany Ferries planned millennium-eve trips with the *Val de Loire* to Rouen and the *Bretagne* to St Malo to take advantage of demand to mark the transition in style.

New ships for the new Millennium

Brittany Ferries' schedules for the 2000 season showed little change from 1999. But the new millennium was marked by a revolutionary new tariff policy for passengers and cars. For the first time for any UK ferry company, the 2000 brochure featured no tariffs, and customers were invited to telephone the company to obtain rates for their journey; the familiar-coloured pricing grids had gone. Whilst this is commonplace today, it represented a revolutionary step in the pre-internet era. The strategy of continued investment in reservations software that characterised the Company's development created the business intelligence that helped build significantly more sophisticated booking processes. Pioneering yield management techniques enabled revenues to be dynamically optimised on each sailing, in a precursor to modern web-based systems. Pricing could now be matched to demand and the revenue for each sailing optimised.

On 8th December 1999 the 37,000-tonne tanker *Erika* left Dunkirk bound for Livorno, Italy with a cargo of 30,884 tonnes of heavy fuel oil. The *Erika* encountered a heavy storm as she entered the Bay of Biscay, and soon found herself in difficulties, listing by ten to twelve degrees to starboard, with water being taken on board and the hull beginning to split. The *Erika* broke her back and started to sink whilst some 30 kilometres south of the Pointe de Penmarc'h in Brittany, despite an attempt to tow her stern section out to sea. Pollution was difficult to contain in the severe weather conditions which, coupled with high tides and currents, caused the slicks to be thrown high up on the shore. Some 400 kilometres of France's coastline was badly affected in another environmental and ecological catastrophe. Whilst memories of the *Amoco Cadiz* had faded, the image of oil-polluted beaches across the western shores of France was an unwelcome feature at the start of the main holiday booking period.

The *Purbeck* spent the winter operating on the Folkestone-Boulogne route and returned on 2nd May to support the *Normandie* and *Duc de Normandie* on the Portsmouth-Caen service. The *Quiberon* maintained the Portsmouth-St Malo route with the *Bretagne,* then operated the winter weekend Plymouth-Roscoff route.

The SEMs' optimism was reflected in the announcement on 27th April of plans for a new ship to be introduced by early 2002. Initial plans to secure Stena Line's *Koningin Beatrix* were thwarted, and the award of a contract by Senacal for the £70 million construction of a new vessel for the Portsmouth-Caen route was confirmed on 11th September. Van der Giessen de Noord of Rotterdam was selected to build a vessel with a specification for up to 175 freight units,

The *Val de Loire* and *Pride of Bilbao* meet each other at the entrance to Portsmouth harbour. *(Ferry Publications Library)*

600 cars and 2,000 passengers, and would deliver the largest ship ever planned for cross-Channel operations, with construction scheduled to start in March 2001. Her capacity was graphically described as being the equivalent of nearly five jumbo jet loads of passengers and a mile and a half of freight vehicles. The finished vessel would incorporate the best of the Van der Giessen de Noord construction methodology, coupled with interior designs by Deltamarin and AIA modelled on the best features of the existing fleet. All cabins would have private facilities and there would be classic Commodore Cabin suites as well as cabins designed specifically for disabled passengers. The design incorporated a choice of restaurants and bars, a club class lounge, and cinemas, coupled with an Internet café and disco designed specifically for teenagers. She would displace the *Duc de Normandie* to the Plymouth-Roscoff service and release the *Quiberon* for sale.

P&O European Ferries' fast craft *SuperStar Express* and her replacement the *Portsmouth Express* was beginning to build a significant niche market. Fast craft were not a core part of the Company strategy and were not considered reliable enough to operate consistently on long distance crossings in the open sea conditions of the western Channel. In September Brittany Ferries released details of a new joint venture with Condor to introduce a high-speed catamaran service between Poole and Cherbourg from the 2001 season. The *Condor Express* and *Condor Vitesse* would run in tandem with the *Barfleur*, crossing to Cherbourg in two hours 15 minutes and featuring a new livery representing both companies. The vessels would be manned by Condor crew and Brittany Ferries' catering staff.

The *Val de Loire* experienced engine problems on 9th September forcing her to be taken out of service and sent to Brest for repairs. The *Bretagne* covered her roster from 16th September and was replaced on her Portsmouth-St Malo duties by the *Duc de Normandie*. The *Barfleur* transferred from Poole to the Portsmouth-Caen service, leaving the *Coutances* and *Purbeck* on a freight-only operation. The *Val de Loire* resumed normal duties on 27th September. The *Purbeck* then moved to serve the Portsmouth-Caen route for winter.

Brittany Ferries made a small profit in 1999/2000; this would have been significantly better if there had not been pollution from the *Erika* in December 1999. The Company's market share in the western Channel sector grew further to 52.6% of the passenger business and 57.7% of freight movements. Passengers carried fell slightly to 2,477,260, and there was a similar drop in vehicle carryings to 657,404, freight shipments recovered to 175,315 units.

Michel Masson announced his resignation as the Company's Directeur Général after 18 months in post on 5th September. During his brief tenure Brittany Ferries had broadly overcome its financial issues and he left the operation in positive financial health. After two external appointments, Masson was replaced by the Company's Chief Financial Officer Michel Maraval. Ian Carruthers also chose to retire from the Company after 19 years driving the strategy from the UK; he left in January 2001, with David Longden taking over his role.

The *Bretagne* underwent a major refit for the fitting of sponsons to her hull between 4th January and 8th March 2001 to allow her to meet the new SOLAS regulations. The Plymouth-Santander route re-started with the *Val de Loire* on 14th March, following the spring re-opening of the Cork-Roscoff service from 9th March. The *Condor Vitesse's* inaugural summer operating season on the Poole-Cherbourg route ran from 22nd May to 30th September.

Meanwhile, the keel for the Company's new Portsmouth-Caen vessel was laid down at the Van der Giessen de Noord shipyard in Rotterdam on 7th June and her name was revealed to be the *Mont St Michel*, after the famous landmark in Brittany. Her design incorporated many aspects of the *Normandie's* general arrangement for her accommodation decks, so that the pair of vessels operating on the same route would offer similar characteristics, thereby simplifying their operation; the *Mont St Michel* differed in having a double funnel casing, which optimised space and capacity on the vehicle deck.

The role of the *Purbeck* in helping to expand freight carryings provided further justification for the impending arrival; traffic grew by 20% following the addition of the chartered vessel to the fleet in Spring 2000, at a time when the market was stagnant elsewhere. The *Mont St Michel* would bring a further 70% uplift in freight capacity, equal to the combined freight capacity of the *Duc de Normandie* and the *Normandie*.

Passenger figures increased by 1.4% in the year to 30th September 2001 to reach 2,581,257, vehicle volumes grew to 688,215, but freight units fell to 168,536. "The return to profit was made in 2001 thanks to a drastic policy of savings and productivity improvements with the withdrawal of a ship from the fleet whilst traffic remained on the rise," explained Maraval at the AGM. The performance of the Poole-Cherbourg fast craft operation exceeded expectations, encouraging the company to retain the chartered service for the 2002 season.

With the *Mont St Michel* project well under way, the team considered the next phase of the fleet renewal programme. The balance of capacity on the Portsmouth-Caen route would be resolved by the arrival of the new vessel, so attention turned to how other routes could be better served. A new Plymouth-based vessel for the Santander and Cork services would provide additional capacity to expand these markets whilst allowing the *Val de Loire* to be cascaded to

Above: **The forward section of the *Mont St. Michel* under construction.** *(Ferry Publications Library)*

Left: **Work advances on the *Mont St Michel* prior to her launch.** *(Ferry Publications Library)*

Below: **The *Mont St Michel* was delayed by her builders for a number of reasons and was eventually launched on 15th March 2002.** *(Ferry Publications Library)*

The *Mont St Michel* leaving Portsmouth shortly after entering service. *(Miles Cowsill)*

The *Condor Vitesse* served on the Poole-Cherbourg service from 2000. The InCat craft is pictured here outward-bound from her Dorset port. *(Kevin Mitchell)*

The *Purbeck*, one of the two original sisters of Truckline, was to have the more varied career. She was chartered to many parts of the world after being cascaded from the Truckline fleet. She is seen here whilst covering freight sailings on the Caen service for Brittany Ferries. *(Miles Cowsill)*

partner the *Bretagne* on the Portsmouth-St Malo route. The project was codenamed 'Bretagne 2' and came to fruition on 22nd February 2002, when an order was placed for the first Northern European car ferry to feature cruise ship facilities, including a swimming pool and cabins with either balconies or terraces. The contract for the 40,589-gt vessel was awarded to the Meyer Werft shipyard at Papenburg, despite pressure from trade unions in France for more local construction. Chantiers de l'Atlantique was unable to meet the delivery deadline, with their workload commitments to build the *Queen Mary 2* for Cunard preventing them being able to deliver a new vessel before April 2004.

Twenty-five per cent of the cost of the new vessel was paid by Sabemen, with the remainder provided on the French Tax Break provisions by a banking pool. To be called *Pont-Aven*, after the town in western Brittany, she would replace the *Val de Loire* on Spanish, French and Irish routes, allowing her to be deployed on the Portsmouth-St Malo operation.

The design of the vessel reflected the combined efforts of Brittany Ferries, Meyer Werft, Deltamarin and AIA to produce a distinctive answer to the challenges of operating to Santander. Maraval was heavily involved in the concept design, seeking to create a vessel that would take the quality of the Spanish route to a different level. The *Pont Aven* would feature a radical new hull form adapted to Bay of Biscay conditions, with a highly curved forward superstructure, a long and low hull, and an angular stern. Her design accommodated 2,415 passengers, 650 cars or up to 85 lorries, with 650 cabins across eight different grades. With a length of

Mont St Michel

Above: **The very well-appointed Les Romantiques dining room which can seat up to 202 passengers.** *(Mike Louagie)*

Top left: **The port-side arcade is furnished to a very high standard.** *(Mike Louagie)*

Bottom left: **La Galerie self-service restaurant situated on Deck 8.** *(Miles Cowsill)*

Below: **The main reception area is modelled on that of the Normandie but clearly has a more modern 'feel' being some ten years later in design and build.** *(Mike Louagie)*

An early artist's impression of the *Pont-Aven*. *(Ferry Publications Library)*

A regular morning sight at St Malo as the *Bretagne* slowly moves out of the port on her morning sailing to Portsmouth. *(Miles Cowsill)*

The *Barfleur* in the evening sunshine outward bound for Cherbourg off Sandbanks, Poole. From November 2007 she ran in tandem with the *Cotentin*. *(Miles Cowsill)*

184.3 metres and a 31-metre-beam, and a service speed of 27 knots she could reduce the 24-hour crossing time between Plymouth and Santander to under 20 hours from Spring 2004.

However, a fast ship of this specification would be expensive to operate, and there were internal concerns about the size of the passenger market for such a vessel and its flexibility of operation between routes.

The *Condor Vitesse* returned to Poole in May, offering a 135-minute crossing to Cherbourg, the fastest crossing on the western Channel. With schedules operating in conjunction with the *Barfleur*, passengers could take an early morning crossing aboard the *Condor Vitesse* and enjoy a full day in Cherbourg before returning to Poole on the *Barfleur*.

Progress continued when the *Mont St Michel* was launched in Rotterdam at 07:00 on 15th March 2002, but her delivery date slipped beyond the original plan of 5th July. The shipyard had produced an over-competitive bid and encountered significant financial problems during the construction phase, requiring refinancing of the business and the installation of a new management team. This forced a shuffling of vessels for the peak season, with the *Quiberon* remaining in service and moving to Portsmouth after her first sailing from Caen on 10th July, having sailed from Plymouth to Caen that morning. The *Duc de Normandie* made the reverse move the previous day to take up station on the Plymouth-Roscoff route and offer an increase in capacity of 15% for passengers and 17% for vehicles on the service compared to the *Quiberon*. The *Quiberon* and *Normandie* soon settled into their new sailing pattern.

The *Oscar Wilde* loads at Cherbourg for Rosslare as the *Barfleur* slips in behind her from Poole. *(Ferry Publications Library)*

For the winter, the *Val de Loire* and *Bretagne* operated on the Portsmouth-St Malo route, with the former also undertaking a St Malo-Plymouth-Cherbourg schedule. The *Duc de Normandie* remained on the Plymouth-Roscoff service. The *Quiberon* and *Normandie* were to maintain the service until the *Mont St Michel* was delivered, when the *Quiberon* would be sold.

The *Mont St Michel* was finally handed over on 11th December and entered service between Caen and Portsmouth on 20th December. She could accommodate 2,140 passengers, with accommodation for 808 in cabins, together with 600 cars or 180 freight vehicles. Her interior matched the standards of her predecessors. The central feature was a grand staircase rising through the centre of three decks. She boasted three dining options on the restaurant deck, including a gastrodôme with an à la carte restaurant and a second gourmet restaurant on the port side. The restaurant was decorated with tableaux by Cathy Banneville and Patrick Serc comprising text and images depicting imaginary sea voyages. The cafeteria was adorned with artwork by Yvonne Guégan, Aldo Paolucci, and Franch Vaucelles. Unusually the vessel featured a delicatessen selling Breton produce. At the stern Bernard Bidault created a small club library meeting room; this was truly a class apart from its competitors. The vessel was built to an extremely high standard and fulfilled all the original design criteria. However, the difficult fit-out not only extended the delivery date for the vessel, but also contributed to the continuation of severe financial difficulties for the Van der Giessen de Noord shipyard, which went into administration shortly after delivery of the *Mont St Michel*.

The *Quiberon* was now surplus to requirements and undertook her final Portsmouth-Caen sailing on 20th December before being laid up. She headed to Brest for an extensive refit after being sold to Medmar/Linee Lauro, leaving Brest on 14th May 2003 as the *Giulia d'Abundo*.

With sales of €322.3 million and a net profit of more than €13 million in 2002, Brittany Ferries was able to celebrate passenger traffic up by four per cent to reach 2,670,363, with vehicles rising to 718,328 and freight units reaching 170,352.

brittanyferries.com
MONT ST MICHEL
Brittany Ferries

The *Mont St Michel* leaving Portsmouth for Caen. The same hull design was used for construction of the *Cotentin* and the *Armorique* (II). *(Miles Cowsill)*

Above: **The funnel of the *Pont-Aven* painted as a priority by her builders.** *(Brian Smith)*

Top right and bottom: **The *Pont-Aven* pictured in the final stages of external construction prior to painting.** *(Brian Smith)*

Below: **Le Café du Festival fitting out.** *(Miles Cowsill)*

Opposite page: **In a clockwise direction from the top: The *Pont-Aven* on her final float out before her passage down the River Ems, approaching the lock on the river to the North Sea at Emssperrwerk, the *Pont-Aven* passes close to the town of Weener and the vessel's first float-out from her construction shed.** *(Miles Cowsill and Brian Smith)*

PONT-AVEN
RADBOD

Brittany Ferries

PONT-AVEN
Brittany Ferries
PONT-AVEN

The ***Pont-Aven*** **arriving at Santander from Portsmouth.** *(Miles Cowsill)*

PONT-AVEN
PONT-AVEN
MORLAIX

Pont-Aven

Above: **Le Grand Pavois bar.** *(Brittany Ferries)*

Top right: **Le Flora restaurant.** *(Brittany Ferries)*

Bottom right: **Le Café du Festival.** *(Brittany Ferries)*

Left: **Atrium.** *(Brittany Ferries)*

Below: **Les Finistères Bar and pool.** *(Brittany Ferries)*

A new weekend link between Plymouth and Cherbourg for winter 2002/3 was provided by the *Duc de Normandie*. It had originally been planned that the *Val de Loire* would take these sailings but instead she boosted capacity on the Portsmouth-St Malo route with the *Bretagne*.

The keel of the new *Pont-Aven* was laid at the Meyer Werft shipyard on 9th April 2003 and building proceeded quickly in anticipation of delivery in spring 2004. On her arrival, plans were prepared for the *Bretagne* to open a new Portsmouth-Cherbourg service, in competition with P&O Ferries whose services to the port had been reduced. If this route proved to be a success, there was an option to build a second *Mont St Michel* and re-allocate the *Normandie* to expand the Portsmouth-Cherbourg route.

The agreement with Condor for the operation of the *Condor Vitesse* alongside the *Barfleur* on the Poole-Cherbourg service was renewed for another season. Meanwhile, P&O Ferries announced plans to operate a new fast craft service between Portsmouth and Caen (Ouistreham) from 2nd April to 30th September 2004, using the 91-metre long Incat fast craft *Max Mols*, which would be renamed the *Caen Express*. Brittany Ferries would face direct competition on this route for the first time.

The *Pont-Aven* was floated out at Meyer Werft on Saturday 13th September, when Gourvennec, Michel Maraval, and Henri-Jean Lebeau, jointly pressed the button to open the dock gate valves and admit 100 million litres of water into the building dock. and moved within the shipyard's covered building dock to be made ready for engine trials and final outfitting. She

left the Papenburg shipyard for sea trials ahead of schedule on 7th February 2004, fitting out at Eemshaven before her handover to Brittany Ferries on 27th February. She then headed for Roscoff, pausing to call in Ouistreham during the journey, and arriving on 2nd March to undertake berthing trials, further fitting out, staff training and her christening ceremony.

Her facilities quickly impressed. AIA were heavily involved with interior design from the start, with Bernard Bidault, Jean-Hubert Mignot and Luc Millequant determining the appropriate décor for each of the passenger spaces on the vessel. The result was a carefully muted use of light and colour to create an ambience consistent with her deployment on the lengthy crossings to Spain. The abstract work of renowned Breton artist François Dilasser was used to decorate the vessel, with much use of natural light to create an internal feeling of spaciousness. The central feature of an atrium spanning four decks became the focal point for the passenger facilities. Cabin accommodation was spread across Deck 5, 6 and 8, with the Commodore Class accommodation on the highest level. Deck 7 hosted a range of dining

The *Pont-Aven* swings off the harbour wall at Roscoff as she leaves for Cork on her overnight sailing to Ireland. *(Brittany Ferries)*

The morning sun catches the *Coutances* as she swings off Brownsea Castle for Cherbourg. *(Miles Cowsill)*

The *Duc de Normandie* seen leaving the berth at Plymouth during her first couple of weeks in service on the Roscoff route following her transfer from the Caen link on the introduction of the *Mont St Michel*. *(Miles Cowsill)*

Prior to entering service the *Pont-Aven* underwent a series of trials to test her capabilities for her role in the Bay of Biscay and Irish Sea. *(Brittany Ferries)*

opportunities from the Viennoisserie 'Le Café du Festival' with views over the bow of the ship, to the self-service restaurant 'La Belle Angèle' with flamenco sculptures by Gérard Venturelli, the 'Fastnet' piano bar and the à la cart restaurant 'La Flora' in the stern which took full advantage of picture windows on three sides and was decorated in Art Nouveau style. The comprehensive retail area 'La Boutique' was situated on Deck 8, with the two-deck show lounge 'Le Grand Pavois' forward of this. There were extensive outdoor areas, which included the Les Finstères swimming pool with a nautical theme, which celebrated the Breton, Spanish, British and Irish bagpipes, representing the links between the cultures of the destinations served by the *Pont Aven*.

The *Pont-Aven* visited Plymouth on 17th March and made her maiden departure with the 23:15 Roscoff-Plymouth sailing on 23rd March. Her first departure from Plymouth to Santander took place the following day, and her accelerated compromise of a 23-hour passage schedule commenced from 4th April. This added resilience to the service without incurring the higher fuel consumption of the dramatically quicker schedule originally envisaged.

P&O Ferries introduced their fast ferry Portsmouth-Caen service as scheduled, but this was short-lived, operating for just one season, and made little difference to Brittany Ferries' operations as the rival service created its own niche market. Brittany Ferries fought back with the opening of the new midweek Portsmouth-Cherbourg service on 5th April using the *Val de Loire* and *Bretagne*. The schedule was not popular and attracted very little traffic. The summer season was again noted for dramatic fare reductions on the short-sea sector; Eurotunnel, for example, reduced its lead-in return fare from £239 to £100 from 28th May. This was to have a significant impact on the Company's fortunes.

The *Pont-Aven* lost two weeks of operation from 10th August after a faulty valve allowed 1,200 tonnes of seawater to flood the auxiliary engine room. The incident happened at Plymouth, when the sea water gate valve failed during a routine filter change. Such was the ingress of water that a marine services tug had to be summoned to pump out the affected space in the vessel. Fully booked return trips to Santander and Roscoff, and the weekend sailings between Roscoff and Cork were cancelled. The *Duc de Normandie* diverted to Poole as the stricken *Pont-Aven* blocked the linkspan in Plymouth. Losses to the Company were said to exceed £6 million following this incident, and Brittany Ferries sought compensation from Meyer Werft. The *Pont-Aven* was sent to Brest for repair; she headed back to Plymouth from the shipyard, but two of her four generators failed shortly after leaving Brest, forcing her to be sent back to Brest for further repairs. She

An interesting view of the *Duc de Normandie* swinging off the entrance to Roscoff harbour. *(Brittany Ferries)*

returned to service to operate at a reduced speed but was withdrawn again after two days for further works.

The *Pont-Aven* was deployed on the Portsmouth-St Malo route at the start of the winter season, despite resistance to the switch from Plymouth, but was forced to operate as a stern loading vessel when further problems required her bow door to be welded shut. She was withdrawn from service on 18th November following a further series of technical problems and headed to Dunkirk for drydocking and replacement of her damaged alternators. The problems were resolved during her refit, which allowed the *Pont-Aven* to operate normally from the New Year.

The *Duc de Normandie* completed her last sailing on the Plymouth-Roscoff route on 30th September and sailed to Ouistreham to discharge. She was laid up in Caen, before returning to Portsmouth on 17th November and heading to the Gdansk shipyard for the fitting of a new sprinkler system, prior to a potential sale.

The price war experienced in the financial year 2003/4 saw Brittany Ferries suffer a 3.9% drop in passenger numbers to 2.53 million, with the tourist vehicle traffic down by three per cent to 754,936.

Brittany Ferries entered the fast ferry business in 2005 with the InCat craft *Normandie Express*. She was chartered initially and later purchased in 2007. *(FotoFlite)*

However, there was continued growth in the freight market, which saw an eight per cent increase in traffic to 204,291 trailers. Although turnover fell by 4.1% to €346.6 million, the Company was able to publish a consolidated net profit of €19.5 million. Fortunately, the company received a payment of some €15.06 million from the international oil fuel compensation fund for losses following the grounding of the tanker *Erika* in 2004.

P&O Ferries' western Channel operations had consistently lost substantial sums of money since the introduction of the former 'Olau' vessels in 1994. The British company's contrasting strategy of relying on chartered rather than owned tonnage burdened the local operation with excessive costs. Consolidating management of the routes from Portsmouth to Dover had little impact and the position was increasingly unsustainable. P&O Ferries announced plans to close the routes from Portsmouth to Le Havre, Caen, and Cherbourg, and from Rosslare to Cherbourg, with the *Pride of Cherbourg*, *Cherbourg Express*, and *Caen Express* all withdrawn from the sector. Formal discussions were initiated with Brittany Ferries to explore options to transfer the *Pride of Portsmouth* and *Pride of Le Havre* (which would be renamed *Étretat* and *Honfleur*), together with the crews of both ships and some shore staff, to French control, with these vessels remaining on the Portsmouth-Le Havre route until 2007; the *Pride of Bilbao* would continue operating independently for P&O Ferries from Portsmouth to Bilbao. Brittany Ferries were keen to see greater price stability and recognised that there were benefits from a single operation with the planned reduction in capacity bringing a more stable business.

The business was eventually offered to Brittany Ferries for €1, with the costs of a further six-month charter of the two 'Olau' ships also covered. But there were still significant issues on pension obligations and the Transfer of Undertakings Protection of Employment (TUPE) legislation, which would safeguard the employment conditions of the former P&O staff, that needed to be resolved. The Office of Fair Trading (OFT) in the UK investigated the proposed takeover and decided against approval of P&O Ferries' proposals. This prompted Brittany Ferries to withdraw from the proposed agreement between the companies.

A disappointed P&O Ferries announced they would close their Le Havre route in September 2005. More immediately, the Portsmouth-Cherbourg route closed after the final sailing of the *Pride of Cherbourg* on 2nd January 2005. Brittany Ferries immediately covered this gap in French services with a revived Portsmouth-Cherbourg route which commenced operation from 2nd January, with the *Normandie*; the *Val de Loire* later joined the winter service on the route.

Meanwhile, Brittany Ferries addressed the niche market for faster services from Portsmouth when the InCat fast craft *Normandie Express* was acquired for the summer season from 16th March. She would provide capacity for 900 passengers and 280 cars, on

PONT-AVEN
MORLAIX

The *Pont-Aven* pictured on the River Seine en route to Rouen. *(Pascal Bredel)*

The *Coutances* discharges her freight at Cherbourg in June 2007. She was transferred to the Portsmouth-Caen service following the introduction of the *Cotentin* on the Poole route in November 2007. *(Miles Cowsill)*

two roundtrip midweek sailings each day between Portsmouth and Cherbourg, offering additional capacity on the Caen route at weekends. The *Normandie Express* sailed from Hobart on 22nd January travelling via Indonesia to deliver aid to areas devastated by the Boxing Day 2004 tsunami.

The *Barfleur* operated a Poole-Cherbourg-Portsmouth-Cherbourg-Poole rotation to incorporate the new Portsmouth route for the summer season, instead of a roster of two Poole-Cherbourg sailings each day. The *Normandie* and *Mont St Michel* maintained the Portsmouth-Caen service, with the *Val de Loire* running on Portsmouth-St Malo, operating overnight from Portsmouth, and returning by day. The *Bretagne* replaced the *Duc de Normandie* on the Plymouth-Roscoff service, operating with the *Pont-Aven*. The Cork-Roscoff route re-opened from 1st April with the *Pont-Aven*, although she was to suffer from further technical issues during her first full year of operation. The *Normandie Express* operated consistently across the summer with no interruptions to service. She provided valuable addition capacity on the Portsmouth-Caen route during peak weekends and achieved good levels of business on both that and the Cherbourg route.

The *Duc de Normandie* was sold to Trans Europa Ferries in March 2005. She arrived in Oostende on 14th March and was renamed the *Wisteria* before heading to the Mediterranean.

Michel Maraval resigned as Managing Director on 3rd August. Alexis Gourvennec was gradually reduced his own day-to-day responsibilities and created a new directoire comprising of Jean-Michel Giguet, Martine Nicolas, and David Longden to take the Company forward. This group became responsible for directing the entire business. Martine Nicolas looked after the finances, Jean-Michel Giguet assumed accountability for all on board services and to a lesser extent the crew, and David Longden was responsible for everything else across the business. The structure began to create a single management team, irrespective of geography, and broke down barriers across the Channel.

The following day Brittany Ferries announced the construction of a new vessel for the Plymouth-Roscoff route by the Aker yards in Helsinki. The new vessel, given the project name 'Coutances 2', after the vessel which she would replace, was scheduled for delivery in 2007. She would measure 165 metres in length and boast deck capacity of 2,200 lane-metres, with accommodation comprising of 120 cabins. The contract price totalled €80 million, with an option for a second vessel. This purchase was supported by Senamanche, with Brittany Ferries agreeing to lease the vessel for 25 years.

P&O Ferries closed their Portsmouth-Le Havre route on 30th September, with the final sailing leaving the French port at 16:30. Within three days the route had been taken up by a new company, LD Lines, a subsidiary of the Louis Dreyfus Armateurs shipping and logistics group, utilising the former P&O Ferries vessel *Pride of Aquitaine* renamed as the *Norman Spirit*.

The 2004-5 season was another success, helped by the demise of P&O Ferries' western Channel services. Passenger numbers grew by 8.8% to reach 2.46 million, and freight carryings rose by 10.1% to 232,723 units.

Farewell Val de Loire, welcome Armorique

Ferry company DFDS had long expressed an interest in acquiring the *Val de Loire*, and they made several attempts to interest the Company in a sale over a two-year period. Although she had been heavily modified from the outset for the Plymouth-Santander route, the *Val de Loire* had not proved to be a good ship in bad weather. The approach represented a good opportunity to dispose of her and DFDS had a surplus vessel to act as a stop gap until a new vessel could be made available. The *Dana Anglia* was not the most appropriate of vessels but would be a suitable, if short-term, charter; a three-year deal gave time for Brittany Ferries to build another ship for the route. The transaction was completed on 25th November, and the vessel named *Pont l'Abbé* after the capital of Pays Bigouden in Finistère.

It did not take long for Brittany Ferries to announce plans for a new vessel to replace the *Val de Loire*. The 'Armorique 2' project envisaged a new ship modelled on the successful *Mont St Michel* design, built by the Aker shipyard in Helsinki. With delivery planned for 2008, she would be completed in time to replace the charter of the *Pont l'Abbé* on the Plymouth-Roscoff route.

The *Val de Loire* made her final sailing on the Portsmouth-Cherbourg route on 20th February 2006 and was handed over to DFDS to operate as the renamed *King of Scandinavia*. The *Pont l'Abbe* took up the Portsmouth-Cherbourg service on 6th March and transferred to the Plymouth-Roscoff service on 31st March, allowing the *Bretagne* to return home to the Portsmouth-St Malo route.

The 20th anniversary of the Portsmouth-Caen service was celebrated on 6th June 2006 with the route's purpose-built *Normandie* and *Mont St Michel* dressed overall for the event. For the late autumn

The *Val de Loire* leaves Portsmouth during her last few days in service with the Company, prior to her sale to DFDS. *(Miles Cowsill)*

The *Pont l'Abbe* at Roscoff loading for her afternoon sailing to Plymouth. *(Miles Cowsill)*

The *Cotentin* entered commercial service on 26th November 2007; she undertook her first sailing to Spain four days later. *(Miles Cowsill)*

The *Normandie Express* passes the *Queen Mary 2* as she leaves Cherbourg. *(Ferry Publications Library)*

services, the *Bretagne* was transferred to the Plymouth-Santander route, while the *Pont-Aven* switched to the Portsmouth-St Malo link for the remainder of the year. In November Brittany Ferries announced that their new ship for their Roscoff-Plymouth service would be named *Armorique* in recognition of the distinguished career of her namesake predecessor. At New Year, the *Pont-Aven* was employed on a special cruise between Portsmouth and Rotterdam.

Sadly, neither Christian Michielini nor Alexis Gourvennec were able to enjoy the long healthy retirement that their contributions to Brittany Ferries' success richly deserved. Alexis Gourvennec died on 19th February 2007 and Christian Michielini followed less than a year later, on 30th January 2008.

The *Bretagne* made her debut on the Poole-Cherbourg route on 27th February 2007, whilst the *Barfleur* underwent her annual overhaul. The fleet carried out a similar pattern of sailings for 2007 to the previous year.

The new freight vessel *Cotentin* was floated out on 12th April following the keel being laid down on 29th November 2006. As the new vessel fitted out in Finland, plans were unveiled for her to be deployed on a new 27-hour weekend freight-only service between Poole and Santander. The £50 million *Cotentin* underwent trials from the yard in Finland during the last week of September, prior to being handed over to Brittany Ferries at the end of October. She entered commercial service on 26th November 2007, undertaking her first trip to Spain on 30th November. Her 23-knot speed enabled a 27-hour crossing time on this service, whilst

The ***Armorique*** **(II) pictured during her final stages of construction in Finland.** *(Ferry Publications Library)*

offering capacity for 200 passengers and 120 freight vehicles. The *Cotentin* was registered in Cherbourg. Poole Harbour Commissioners spent some £6.5 million dredging the port to facilitate operation of the new vessel.

The winter pattern of operations was to a see a similar roster to that of 2006/2007, with the *Pont-Aven* and *Bretagne* swapping routes. The *Bretagne* acted as winter refit cover for the *Mont St Michel* and *Normandie* on the Caen route and the *Pont l'Abbe* at Plymouth. The latter was purchased from DFDS on 21st December. Meanwhile, the keel of the new *Armorique* was laid in early November.

The *Normandie Express* spent a fortnight operating the Plymouth-Roscoff route in February 2008 as refit cover for the *Pont l'Abbe* in an unusual winter deployment. The *Coutances* completed made her final sailing for Brittany Ferries from Poole on 26th April and was laid up in Cherbourg from 1st May; she had completed over 36,000 crossings of the English Channel during her career with Truckline and Brittany Ferries.

A fishermen's dispute brough some disruption to services in late May and early June, with the *Barfleur* operating from Poole to Roscoff for a short period.

The new £90 million *Armorique* was launched at the Aker shipyard in Helsinki on 10th August. Designed specifically for the Plymouth-Roscoff-Cork services, she had capacity for 1,500 passengers and 500 cars, and a service speed of 23 knots. Equipped with 247 en-suite cabins, the Armorique also featured reserved seating lounges and an open plan layout. Her modern design featured décor to capture the light, colour and

The *Bretagne* made her debut on the Poole-Cherbourg service in February 2007. *(Kevin Mitchell)*

The *Pont-Aven* covered the St Malo link on several occasions during the winter periods. She is seen here leaving the Breton port in November 2007. *(Miles Cowsill)*

ARMORIQUE
MORLAIX
KRAFT

The *Armorique* leaving Finland on her delivery voyage to Brest. *(Ferry Publications Library)*

Armorique

Above: **Reception Area.** *(Miles Cowsill)*

Top right: **Lounge Cafe.** *(Miles Cowsill)*

Bottom right: **Self-service restaurant on Deck 7.***(Miles Cowsill)*

Below: **Main Garage/Freight Deck.** *(Miles Cowsill)*

space of the Brittany region and its maritime heritage, hosting Breton artists' work celebrating regional culture, traditions, spirit, and innovation.

As financial institutions experienced turbulent trading conditions following the collapse of Lehman Brothers on 15th September, a global recession sparked a downturn in business. The *Normandie Express* was withdrawn from service early on 30th September as a fuel saving measure. The rising cost of fuel put on hold plans to deploy the *Pont-Aven* on the Portsmouth-St Malo and a new Portsmouth-Santander route from 2009. Her retention at Plymouth would permit the disposal of the *Pont l'Abbe*.

During 2008 Brittany Ferries carried 2,733,655 passengers, a rise of some 2.8% on the previous year, and car traffic overall increased by some 6.4%. Freight levels dropped as the global economic crisis began to bite in the last quarter of trading.

The winter of 2008/9 saw the *Bretagne* undergo an £8 million refurbishment and refit in Poland in readiness for the 2009 season, her 20th year of service with Brittany Ferries. She returned to the Portsmouth-St Malo route on 17th March. The new *Armorique* underwent sea trials in mid-December 2008 and left Finland on 27th January for Brest, for further fit-out and a period of staff training, prior to entering service from Roscoff to Plymouth on 11th February 2009, delayed by 24 hours after the intervention of severe weather. Unusually for Brittany Ferries her bespoke design for the Plymouth-Roscoff route did not feature a restaurant, as her schedule was not conducive to justifying the expense of provision. This caused some controversy both within and outside the Company.

The *Pont-Aven* opened a new Portsmouth-Santander service on 18th March 2009, with a 24-hour passage time. With continued growth of the UK-Spanish services, the dedicated freight vessel *Cotentin* increased her sailings from Poole to Santander to two round sailings a week.

In December 2009 Brittany Ferries announced the purchase of the Greek-owned *Superfast V* for additional tonnage on the Santander and Cherbourg services. With a service speed of 23 knots, the new ferry was ideal for her new role from Portsmouth, boasting two large car and freight decks and two lower holds for cars – an overall capacity of 712 cars/77 lorries. Brittany Ferries took delivery of the *Superfast V* in February 2010, renaming her *Cap Finistère* for her new role. Considerable work was undertaken to the vessel's interior to bring her in line with rest of the fleet, the most apparent refurbishment being the central casino area to convert it into a self-service café, Petite Marché. The new ship entered service in March.

Many aircraft were grounded in the week ending 22nd April 2010, when an erupting volcano in Iceland threw a huge cloud of ash into the air, generating an additional 35,000 foot-passengers for Brittany Ferries, more than five times the corresponding week of 2009, as stranded travellers headed to Europe's key continental ferry ports in a bid to find an alternative way home.

In September 2010, in the light of continued losses, P&O Ferries closed its last remaining western Channel service, the route from Portsmouth to Bilbao. Brittany Ferries responded by announcing that the Company would supplement its existing services and fill the void on the Bilbao route, twice a week in 2011, with the *Cap Finistère,* and offer up to five return sailings each week to the Iberian Peninsula in total.

In March 2011 Brittany Ferries and shipbuilder STX France revealed that they were embarking on a new joint study project to develop a new generation of environmentally friendly passenger ferries. The new ships, powered by dual-fuel engines, were planned to

In December 2009 Brittany Ferries announced the purchase of the Greek-owned *Superfast V* for additional tonnage on the Santander and Cherbourg services. *(Ferry Publications Library)*

Brittany Ferries took delivery of the *Superfast V* in February 2010, renaming her the *Cap Finistère* for her new role. *(Miles Cowsill)*

Part of the retail shop area on the *Cap Finistère*. *(Miles Cowsill)*

The attractive two tier aft bar on the *Cap Finistère*. *(Miles Cowsill)*

burn liquefied natural gas (LNG) in combination with a high-efficiency electric propulsion system, reducing energy consumption and CO2 emissions by 15-20% compared with the current ferries.

On 27th March the *Cap Finistère* opened the new Portsmouth-Bilbao service, marking Brittany Ferries' first new port destination for some 25 years. The expanded service pattern to Spain brought further growth, despite the global recession, although trade on the UK-France links showed a small decline due to the strength of the Euro and the overall drop in trade within the Eurozone. Although recording a 7% increase in turnover in 2010/11, Brittany Ferries made an €18 million loss, with Sterling's decreasing value against the Euro being a major contributory factor. With 85% of the Company's traffic, totalling 2.6 million passengers 800,000 cars and 200,000 freight units, coming from Britain and revenue received in sterling, this posed an increasing problem for the Company.

The *Bretagne* went to Cherbourg to de-store on 24th November 2011, and then sailed to Le Havre for lay-up through the winter period, to re-enter service on the Portsmouth-St Malo route on 29th March 2012. The *Barfleur* spent the winter laid up in Caen, whilst the *Normandie Express* was laid up in Cherbourg. In May 2012 the *Normandie* chalked up her 20th year of service on the Portsmouth-Caen link, having lost very few sailings during her long career. It was estimated at the time that she had travelled 2.2 million miles – almost the equivalent of five return trips to the moon.

These were difficult times. There was to be no Poole-Cherbourg conventional passenger service in 2012 following a sustained period of weak demand,

A publicity view taken off Cherbourg with the ***Normandie Express*****, *Cotentin*** **and** ***Cap Finistère*****.** *(Brittany Ferries)*

An impressive view of the *Cap Finistère* arriving early on her overnight sailing from Portsmouth at Santander with the pilot boat in attendance. The vessel proved an excellent timekeeper on the Spanish route during career with Company. *(Miles Cowsill)*

CAP FINISTERE
CAP FINISTERE

The *Cap Finistère* at speed in the English Channel. *(FotoFlite)*

The ***Barfleur*** is seen here as the ***Deal Seaways*** whilst on charter to DFDS for their Dover-Calais link. The ***Pride of Canterbury*** is astern of the ***Deal Seaways***. *(FotoFlite)*

The ***Cotentin*** leaves Santander for Poole for the last time in October 2013, prior to her charter to Stena Line. *(Miles Cowsill)*

The former ***Cotentin*** is seen here as the ***Stena Baltica***, arriving at Gdynia from Karlskrona. *(Frank Lose)*

with the *Barfleur* chartered for six months to LD Lines/DFDS as the *Deal Seaways* for use on Dover-Calais services following the demise of the SeaFrance operation at Calais, manned by an LD Lines French crew. The joint fast craft operation with Condor on the Cherbourg route was terminated at the end of the season in September 2012, after eleven years. Brittany Ferries planned to re-open the route to passengers on a more limited basis in 2013, with the *Barfleur* scheduled to make one round-trip sailing each day.

The struggle to find a solution to the financial problems led to a difficult summer of wildcat strikes in protest at cost savings and working practice changes. In a repeat of previous reactions to such activity, the Company withdrew all services on 21st September and laid-up the fleet pending an agreement with the workforce on a way forward. The *Cotentin, Mont St Michel* and the *Normandie Express* went to Cherbourg for lay-up, whilst the *Normandie* used her berth at Caen, and the *Bretagne* was halted at St Malo. The *Pont-Aven* went to Brest to be laid-up and the *Armorique* found herself at Roscoff. The *Cap Finistère* remained at Santander until the industrial action could be resolved. Agreement with trade unions was eventually reached on 1st October and the fleet gradually returned to normal operations from the following day.

The Company's 40th anniversary celebrations on 3rd January 2013 were more muted than might have been the case, reflecting the prevailing economic climate. The new agreement with trade unions led to the *Normandie Express* dropping her weekend trips to Caen, offering only daily Portsmouth-Cherbourg return sailings between 17th May and 9th September 2013. The Poole-Cherbourg fast-craft service operated by Condor was replaced by the *Barfleur* from 18th March as planned, with one daily rotation, and enjoyed good loadings, encouraging a return to near year-round sailings from 2014. The Portsmouth-St Malo service was reduced by one sailing each way per week during the off-peak period, and there were service reductions on the two-ship Portsmouth-Caen service. The *Cotentin* was retained on the twice-weekly Poole-Santander freight link until this closed on 30th September and was then then laid up prior to a charter to Stena Line to operate between Gdynia and Karlskrona. Passenger services to Spain and Roscoff were unaffected by these cost-saving service reductions.

All was not doom and gloom. A new fast craft-operated Portsmouth-Le Havre route was launched on 16th May 2013, with the *Normandie Express* running four days a week in tandem with a rescheduling of the Portsmouth-Cherbourg service at weekends; the new service operated until 8th September.

Amidst the difficult trading conditions Brittany Ferries continued to take the long-term view, and there was more positive news when the Company ordered a new 52,500-gt LNG-powered ferry on 14th January 2014 to replace the *Pont-Aven* on the Plymouth/Portsmouth-Santander and Roscoff-Cork services on delivery in late spring 2017. Under the project name of Pegasus, the construction of the vessel was awarded to STX France at their yard at Santander. The vessel, with a length of 210 metres, was planned to have a service speed of 25 knots and carry up to 650 cars and 2,400 passengers in 649 cabins. Her arrival would allow the *Pont-Aven* to transfer to the Portsmouth-St Malo service and replace the 1989-built *Bretagne*. There were also plans to upgrade the *Armorique, Mont St Michel,* and *Pont-Aven* to operate on more climate-friendly LNG fuel.

However, in early November 2014 the Company announced that plans to upgrade the fleet to operate on LNG, and the new ship ordered under Project Pegasus were all put on hold. The economic viability of the project, which required a heavy financial investment, had been undermined by the Company's inability to secure a temporary exemption for the use of diesel oil instead of heavy fuel oil until the ships had been converted. Instead, the three vessels would be fitted with scrubber technology, in a programme costing between €70 and €80 million. The Company began to look at other ways to secure a replacement for the much-loved *Bretagne*, including building a conventional diesel ship or the purchase of a second-hand vessel. This decision gave the *Bretagne* an extended period with the fleet, and she continued to burn diesel oil.

Meanwhile Brittany Ferries took a two-year charter of the former *Norman Voyager*, renamed *Étretat*, from Stena Line to introduce a new 'no frills' service between Portsmouth and Le Havre and Santander following the withdrawal of the *Cotentin* for charter, and to counter LD Lines' expansion in the Western Channel. Branded as Brittany Ferries 'Économie', the new product was designed to appeal to those travelling to France and Spain at low cost, without the normal cruise-style experience. This new Santander operation achieved good loadings with both holiday and freight traffic. The weekday Le Havre service proved more difficult to fill, with fierce freight competition from the short sea routes supressing loads across the English Channel.

In 2011 Brittany Ferries and STX Europe announced plans to develop a new generation of ferries. This view shows an artist's impression of the proposed new ferry for Brittany Ferries' Spanish service. *(Brittany Ferries)*

Brittany Ferries enjoyed a record summer in 2014, carrying almost three quarters of a million passengers from Portsmouth to France and Spain during the June-August period. After suffering cumulative losses of some €70 million over the last four years, including €17 million in 2011/12, the company returned to profit in 2012/13, achieving a surplus of €1.6 million. The restructuring plan proved highly effective, the UK economy improved, and the operation of fewer sailings resulted in higher passenger loadings on the fleet. Freight revenue was still down by five per cent, attributed to an intense price war with competitors on the Dover Strait.

The *Bretagne* finished her season on the Portsmouth-St Malo service on 15th October and transferred to Plymouth to cover the Roscoff sailings and the mid-week St Malo route until the end of 2013. She was replaced by the *Pont-Aven* on the St Malo link and later by the *Armorique*. Winter operations on the Spanish routes were covered by the *Pont-Aven, Cap Finistère*, and the *Étretat*.

The autumn saw the first ships undergo work to meet the new emissions policy being introduced by the European Union. The *Normandie* was the first in the fleet to head for scrubber conversion at Santander in a three-month duration programme, and the *Cap Finistère* followed her in mid January. The *Barfleur* continued her Poole-Cherbourg service until 15th March 2015, when she left for her two-month scrubber

The *Norman Voyager* arriving at Le Havre prior to her renaming as the *Étretat*. From March 2014 she was employed on services from Portsmouth to Le Havre and Santander. *(Pascal Bredel)*

The *MN Pelican* swinging off the berth at Poole. The freight-only vessel has a capacity for around 100 unaccompanied trailers and eight drivers, and began service with the Company in February 2016. *(Kevin Mitchell)*

fitment programme, representing a positive £10 million investment in a 23-year-old ferry. The fast craft *Normandie Express* took over Poole-Cherbourg sailings from 30th April until the *Barfleur* returned to service from 16th May. Planning of the investment programme continued through the year with the *Mont St Michel, Pont-Aven,* and *Armorique* continuing to operate on diesel oil in 2015 in advance of their scrubber conversion the following winter. The *Mont St Michel* became the first to have her scrubber technology fitted in late autumn 2015. She was followed by the *Pont-Aven* in January 2016, and the *Armorique* in February 2016.

With the pound strengthening against the Euro and early signs of economic growth returning in Britain, Brittany Ferries had a good trading year on most routes.

The return of the concept of 'Économie' sailings offered by the *Étretat* in 2014 proved very popular, and this success prompted the charter of the former *Dana Serena* from DFDS for a five-year period from May 2015 to expand these no-frills operations. After an extensive refit, the former Harwich-Esbjerg vessel, was scheduled to operate in tandem with the *Étretat* between Portsmouth and Le Havre and operate a weekly 'Économie' sailing to Bilbao. Facilities and space on board were limited for 'Économie' passengers, although the former DFDS Commodore cabins were available as economy plus cabins and the Commodore lounge became a quiet room for reading on board. The vessel was renamed *Baie de Seine* for her new deployment.

The *Étretat* was withdrawn from service in late February due to a stabiliser fault and went for overhaul to Poland. Her place was taken by the *Bretagne*, which was brought out of lay-up to cover the Le Havre and Bilbao services until she opened the St Malo route on 16th March. This closed the 'Économie' passenger service until the entry into service of the *Baie de Seine*; she undertook her first freight sailing between Portsmouth and Bilbao at 08:15 on 9th May and two days later made her first passenger sailing between Portsmouth and Le Havre, departing at 23:15. The vessel offered very comfortable accommodation and was well received by passengers.

Following completion of repairs and the fitting of new stabilisers, the *Étretat* returned to Le Havre on 21st May and re-entered commercial service the next day on the 22:00 sailing to Portsmouth. Meanwhile, the *Normandie Express* re-opened the Portsmouth-Cherbourg route on 29th April and operated to Cherbourg from both Portsmouth and Poole from the following day until 14th May in the absence of the *Barfleur*.

On 6th May, dockers strategically parked trailers on the *Mont St Michel's* ramp as passengers were boarding at Caen for the 08:40 sailing to Portsmouth, to prevent it from being closed, in a further round of industrial action. Passengers disembarked, but the *Mont St Michel* was unable to leave port, forcing the *Normandie* to divert her incoming sailing to Cherbourg. On 10th May around 20 Brittany Ferries shareholders, led by the Chairman, Jean-Marc Roué, liberated the ship; the *Mont St Michel* sailed from Caen, arriving for the first time ever at her home port of Roscoff. The next day the *Normandie* departed from Portsmouth for Cherbourg at 08:15 but was diverted by industrial action to Roscoff, becoming the second ship to visit the port for

The *Sirena Seaways* was chartered to Brittany Ferries in 2015 for five years. Here the renamed *Baie de Seine* leaves Le Havre following her overhaul at the port prior to entering service. *(Pascal Bredel)*

The stylish ***Normandie*** lost her beautiful orginial lines with the re-building of her funnel to accommodate scrubber units. *(Miles Cowsill)*

The ***Pont-Aven*** returned in 2016 from extensive works to provide scrubbers units looking very different with a large funnel. The works were carried out at the Remontowa Shipyard at Gdansk. *(Miles Cowsill)*

In March 2015 the ***Barfleur*** underwent a re-building programme to install scrubber units in her funnels. *(Kevin Mitchell*

Looking a very different 'Superfast' vessel, the ***Cap Finistère*** leaves Portsmouth with her new funnel design following installation of her scrubber unit at Astillero Shipyard, Santander in 2015. *(Miles Cowsill)*

MONT ST MICHEL
MONT ST MICHEL

Mont St Michel *(Miles Cowsill)*

the first time. The strike ended on 13th May.

Brittany Ferries carried a record 506,000 passengers from Portsmouth during the summer months of July and August, an increase of eight per cent on 2014, with all routes performing well. The Plymouth-Roscoff service saw a three per cent increase in passenger levels, with 148,000 passengers using the route and the Poole-Cherbourg service witnessed an increase of 8 per cent. Brittany Ferries carried 838,000 passengers across all its routes, the highest for 13 years. In the year 2014-15, passenger numbers grew by 5.5 per cent to 2,567,298, and freight volumes rose 21 per cent to 186,385 units in the same period. Turnover grew by €56 million or 12 per cent to €467.7 million.

The long refit periods of the *Mont St Michel, Pont-Aven* and *Armorique* necessitated a major operational plan to be put in place to allow all three ships to receive scrubbers and other technical improvements. The Plymouth-Santander service closed from 3rd November 2015 until 27th April 2016. The *Mont St Michel* left the Portsmouth-Caen service on 25th September 2015 for a 75-day stay at the Astander Shipyard in Santander to receive scrubbers and an additional funnel. Brittany Ferries' engineers and naval architects worked hard to achieve an aesthetically pleasing result that complemented the look of the ship. The installation of the new scrubber equipment also necessitated the building of significant amounts of new infrastructure below decks, including the provision of new pump rooms, heating and cooling equipment, storage tanks, and a complete rebuilding of the restaurant.

The *Armorique* and *Pont-Aven* were withdrawn for their scrubber work in Santander and Gdansk respectively, from 4th January 2016, with the Plymouth-Roscoff route closed in their absence until 15th March. Meanwhile, the *Bretagne* operated the St Malo route during January and February 2016. The *Normandie Express* underwent an extensive refit at Dunkirk and appeared in a new livery for 2016.

Growth in freight movements from Spain prompted Brittany Ferries to charter the French vessel *Pelican* from early January 2016, to open a new freight-only route between Poole and Bilbao for an initial period of twelve months, with an optional extension. The 1999-built *Pelican* brought capacity for 100 unaccompanied trailers, with berths for eight freight drivers in three large en-suite cabins. She also freed up capacity on passenger ships during the crucial summer peak season.

The *Armorique's* scrubber conversion work was completed in late February, and she sailed from Santander on 15th March to re-enter commercial operations on 4th April between Plymouth and Roscoff. Her conversion work followed similar lines to the *Mont St Michel*, with an additional central funnel unit housing the French-manufactured insulation. In contrast, the *Normandie, Barfleur,* and *Cap Finistère* all had these

An early artist's impression of the *Honfleur.* *(Brittany Ferries)*

The *Armorique* arriving at Portsmouth following a new scrubber unit being incorporated into her funnel. *(Darren Holdaway)*

units operating within their engine room areas. The *Pont-Aven* was fitted with two smaller scrubber units each side of a large funnel unit, again modelled on the *Mont St Michel* design. The complexity of her work delayed her return from the Polish yard until 27th March, and she re-entered service on 1st April from Roscoff to Cork.

The retirement of Martine Jourdren as Chief Executive Officer after 42 years' service with Brittany Ferries was announced at the company's AGM in early March. In a continuation of the successful policy of promotion from within, Strategy and Commercial Director Christophe Mathieu was appointed as her successor. He was well versed in the Company's operations, having worked on both sides of the Channel.

The *Pont-Aven* experienced problems with one of her controllable pitch propellers whilst on passage between Cork and Roscoff on 7th May and was diverted to Brest. Her 1,000 passengers and their cars were disembarked and the *Pont-Aven* was dry docked at Damen shipyard. The fault was traced to the propeller hub, which in turn had caused the port propeller shaft to malfunction. She did not re-enter service until 26th May, requiring over 10,000 passengers to have their travel arrangements re-organised. A series of strikes at Le Havre and Cherbourg compounded these problems and affected some St Malo sailings.

At celebrations to mark 40 years of cross-Channel ferries from Portsmouth, and 30 years of the route to Caen, chairman Jean-Marc Roué confirmed that the company hoped to place orders for two newbuilds in 2016 to replace the *Bretagne* (1989) and *Normandie* (1992). There was further cause for celebration in mid-April, when Brittany Ferries was voted best ferry operator by passengers in the Daily Telegraph's annual Travel Awards for the third consecutive year.

The outcome of the UK referendum on 24th June 2015, which indicated a majority of voters in favour of leaving the European Union, prompted an initial pledge by Brittany Ferries to continue services as usual. The outcome of the vote created great uncertainty for a Company whose birth had coincided with the UK joining the European Union in 1973. Despite this outcome, the port of Portsmouth recorded a second consecutive record summer for passenger numbers. 828,492 people travelled through Portsmouth from June to August, services from Poole and Plymouth reported a slight decrease in passenger numbers with 319,617 passengers carried. The company reported a record day in its 43-year history on 13th August, when 21,900 passengers were carried across all routes.

The *Normandie Express's* summer season ended on 13th September after which the vessel went to Le Havre for winter lay-up. After the prolonged programme of scrubber fitment, the Company's refit schedule was much less intensive this year.

The *Mont St Michel* played a central role in a British feature film 'The Time of Their Lives' starring Joan Collins and Pauline Collins. Several scenes were shot in Ouistreham, with extensive filming also taking place on board the *Mont St Michel*, as well as in Portsmouth.

In a sign of growing confidence in the continuity of business despite the outcome of the Brexit vote, Brittany Ferries signed a letter of intent on 21st December 2016 with the Flensburger Schiffbau-

Gesellschaft Shipyard (FSG) in Germany, to construct a new ship powered by LNG for the Portsmouth-Caen link. This was seen to be the first step towards a new generation of 'greener' Brittany Ferries ships. The final contract was confirmed on 21st June 2017 at press conference when the name of the new ship was revealed as the *Honfleur* in her namesake town, following the Company's long tradition of naming ships after destinations in France. With capacity for 1,680 passengers in 257 cabins, the vessel would carry 130 freight trailers, or 550 cars and 64 freight trailers on her 2,600-lane metre deck capacity. The £175 million *Honfleur* was planned to enter service in 2019 on the Portsmouth-Caen route alongside *Mont St Michel*, which would allow the displaced *Normandie* to move to expand the Portsmouth-Le Havre service.

The addition of an LNG-powered vessel to the fleet required a new approach to fuel provision, and Brittany Ferries entered a partnership with Total for its delivery. The plan envisaged fuel being transported from LNG terminals in 40-foot containers to meet the *Honfleur* whilst in port in Ouistreham, then driven on board and hoisted into position alongside a fixed LNG storage tank at the rear of the superstructure. This move to LNG fuel followed the completion of the €90 million investment programme in sulphur and particulate-reducing 'scrubber' technology, that had been retrospectively fitted to six Brittany Ferries ships over the previous 18 months; this project was supported by around £5 million in joint funding from the EU and its executive agency INEA, and the ADEME in France.

Poole Harbour Commissioners began work at the end of 2016 to construct a new South Quay at the port. This extension sought to create facilities to accommodate cruise ships and cargo vessels up to 200m in length, the longest the harbour could handle due to the limitations of the shipping channel and turning basin. The construction absorbed 1,700 tons of steel piles, all of which were delivered by sea. The 150,000 cubic metres of sand required for infilling was taken directly from the port's maintenance dredging scheme.

Although Brexit talks between the UK government and its European counterparts had yet to begin, Brittany Ferries and Portsmouth International Port entered a mutual ten-year commitment to strengthen their long-established ties. The contract, the first formal deal of this nature despite a relationship that had now extended for more than 40 years, was signed on board the *Bretagne* by Port Director Mike Sellers and CEO Christophe Mathieu.

At the end of March, the *Cap Finistère* returned to the Portsmouth and Spanish services, following an extensive refit in Santander. Meanwhile, unaccompanied trailer volumes on the Poole-Bilbao service proved encouraging and the *Pelican's* charter was extended for 2018 and 2019.

The *Étretat* awaits her afternoon sailing to Portsmouth at the former P&O Ferries berth located at Quai Auguste Brostrom, Le Havre. *(Pascal Bredel)*

New ship progress -Enter the E-Flexers

With the charter of the DFDS-owned *Baie de Seine* due to expire in April 2019 and no renewal option available, plans for replacement tonnage became a priority. Following the start of a £175 million investment in the new *Honfleur*, the Company confirmed investment in a second new vessel by signing an agreement to charter the third ship in Stena's new E-Flexer sequence of vessels to be built by AVIC Weihai in China. The five-year bareboat charter agreement included an option to extend the charter beyond the initial period or for Brittany Ferries to purchase the ship. The flexibility of the 212 metres x 27.8 metres ro-pax design proved particularly attractive, as it enabled the hull to be adapted to the Company's bespoke requirements. Although retaining the basic configuration of the core E-Flexer series, including deck capacity of 3,100 lane-meters, the plans envisaged the 927-passenger ship being tailored to meet Brittany Ferries' needs, particularly through the provision of additional cabins. The ship would therefore receive typical Brittany Ferries touches and décor and be a recognisable fleet stablemate, albeit to a standard 'shell' design. Although to be built as gas-ready ship, Brittany Ferries elected to install scrubbers on their new build.

Delivery of the new Stena ro-pax was planned for early autumn 2020, some 18 months after the *Baie de Seine* was due to be returned to DFDS. Although the *Baie de Seine* was deployed on both the Le Havre and Bilbao/Santander routes from Portsmouth, Christophe Mathieu indicated that the new vessel would solely be deployed on the Portsmouth-Spain services, although no decision had been taken as to whether the destination port would be Santander or Bilbao. With the *Normandie* set to be displaced on the Portsmouth-Caen route by the new *Honfleur* following her delivery from FSG in June 2019, there were future options to cover the Le Havre

The *Cap Finistère* showing off her clean lines at Le Havre following her repainting in the new livery of the Company. *(Pascal Bredel)*

A further artist's impression of the *Honfleur* sporting the new livery of the Breton company. *(Brittany Ferries)*

The central passenger section of the *Honfleur* is lifted onto the hull of the vessel. *(Brittany Ferries)*

The forward passenger and bridge section of the *Honfleur* is lowered into position. *(Brittany Ferries)*

route with this vessel.

In the light of continued weakness of Sterling against a strong Euro, Brittany Ferries saw a drop in passenger and car traffic to France especially on the routes to Caen and Roscoff. However, the St Malo service was comparatively little affected by currency issues, with car and passenger numbers holding up well. With new tonnage coming on stream on other routes, the 28-year-old *Bretagne* remained a popular fixture on the service despite the route being capable of supporting a larger vessel with more cabin capacity. Brittany Ferries carried 213,000 freight units up to 31st October 2017, an increase of four per cent, but the number of passengers dropped by three per cent to 2,352,000. However, passenger numbers on the longer routes (UK-Spain and France-Ireland) rose by five per cent to 394,000. On the UK-France routes numbers declined by five per cent. The results pointed to tougher trading conditions in the wake of the Brexit vote but confirmed that the company's diversification strategy was working. "There are positive indicators in these results, such as our freight figures, but we can say for sure that Brexit is affecting us commercially and financially," said Christophe Mathieu. "Long routes from the UK to Spain and between France and Ireland have performed well, but passenger traffic from the UK to France has fallen significantly. This is most of our business, and the downturn comes on both sides of the Channel, so a decline in the number of French visitors coming to the UK too. In addition to these challenges our financial results have been affected by the dramatic fall in the value of the pound. Despite this, we remain confident in our diversification strategy. We are also optimistic about the future and are committed to investing in fleet renewal."

Following the arrival of the giant Royal Navy aircraft carrier *HMS Queen Elizabeth* at her new home port of Portsmouth, restrictions were placed on ferry movements to and from the Continental Port, and permission for large ferries to pass each other within the port area was withdrawn. This reduced the flexibility of the timetable in the Portsmouth area.

The European Investment Bank (EIB), Société Générale and Brittany Ferries announced the first green maritime financing package under EIB's €750 million Green Shipping Guarantee (GSG) programme on 11th December 2017. Acquisition of the *Honfleur* would be supported by the bank of the European Union under the GSG programme, which was focused on the environment and climate change. The *Honfleur's* LNG fuelled engines made her an ideal candidate for the scheme. Société Générale acted as the main facilitator of the €142.6 million financing for the acquisition of the *Honfleur*, which included a tranche of €49.5 million fully guaranteed by the EIB. Jean-Marc Roué noted that Brittany Ferries was the first French passenger transport company to pave the way towards energy transition using LNG. He observed that the company operated in four European Union countries, and therefore was truly European with an ambition to lead by example at the top of its priorities, as the recent COP23 requested of both States and businesses.

Brittany Ferries' founder Alexis Gourvennec was commemorated by the unveiling of a memorial stone at the Roscoff terminal on 2 December 2017. The event marked the renaming of the Port du Bloscon in his

The *Connemara* was painted in a hybrid Brittany Ferries livery, keeping her red lower hull with white upper works; a Brittany Ferries logo was placed on the hull and the funnel repainted into fleet livery. *(Pascal Bredel)*

honour—it became known as 'L'Espace Alexis Gourvennec'. Several members of his family were present with local dignitaries at the ceremony; the stone was then moved to its final location at the main entrance to the port.

The keel-laying ceremony for the fleet of new ro-pax vessels being built for Stena RoRo, including the vessel destined to be chartered to Brittany Ferries was held on 2nd February 2018 at the AVIC Weihai Shipyard in China. Meanwhile, construction of the new 42,400-gt *Honfleur* began at the FSG shipyard in Germany on 12th March 2018, when white-hot plasma jets cut through sheets of steel in the formal cutting ceremony. The ship was

The *Baie de Seine* leaves Portsmouth for Bilbao. *(Miles Cowsill)*

Galicia **and** ***Salamanca*** **were the names chosen by Brittany Ferries for their new 'E Flexer'ships for the Spanish services, following a competition among staff after confirmation of the ships' charters from Stena RoRo.** *(Brittany Ferries)*

The ***Armorique*** **arrives at Portsmouth whilst covering the St Malo link.** *(Darren Holdaway)*

The ***Normandie*** **still remains a very modern looking ship at 20 years of age in 2022, which is a compliment to her builders and designers two decades ago.** *(Darren Holdaway)*

expected to take just over a year to complete, with keel laying planned for August, launch in December and sea trials some three months later. The programme still envisaged the *Honfleur* being delivered in May 2019 to allow for trials and training before her first crossing on the Portsmouth-Caen route in June.

Although there was still a lack of clarity as to the new trading arrangements between the UK and the EU following Brexit, Brittany Ferries took a pro-active stance by announcing the first direct ferry link between Ireland and Spain, with the establishment of a twice-weekly Cork-Santander service. The potential for this direct link within the EU had long been mooted, and the port of Cork put considerable effort into securing such a service, but proposals had failed to attract an operator. In 2014 there was briefly a weekly summer connection from Rosslare to Gijon, albeit via St Nazaire, when LD Lines' now defunct Biscay operation from Gijon to St Nazaire was expanded with the addition of a second vessel. The new service enabled freight carriers to bypass established Landbridge routes from Ireland through the UK to continental Europe by sailing direct on an intra-EU service thereby avoiding potential bureaucracy and any delays associated with any Brexit-related customs and immigration processes. With over two million annual tourist visits from Ireland to Spain and 400,000 travelling the other way, the service also held attraction to passengers during the summer. By being the first in the market and quickly commencing operations, Brittany Ferries sought to deter other carriers from entering the market.

The *Asterion*, a Stena RoRo-owned Visentini ro-pax, which latterly sailed for ANEK Lines between Venice and Patras, was taken on charter for the new route. A close sister to Brittany Ferries' *Étretat*, the vessel was no stranger to Santander, having operated for LD Lines as the *Norman Asturias*. The 2007-built 26,500-gt vessel boasted a speed of 24 knots and was to be named the *Stena Ausonia* but became the *Borja* for Baleària on completion. She had accommodation for 500 passengers with berths for 480 in 120 cabins, carried 190 cars and had deck capacity of 2,255 lane metres. In a first for Brittany Ferries, the non-French name of *Connemara* was chosen for the renamed vessel, reflecting the fact that she was not French-crewed or flagged. The company reached agreement with the Workers Council to permit the vessel to operate under the Cypriot flag for a maximum of two years and help keep the start-up costs of operation to an acceptable level to allow the route to develop. However, the French Trade Union CFDT reacted angrily to the proposal, accusing Brittany Ferries of 'social dumping'.

As with the *Étretat*, sailings were marketed under the 'Économie' brand, with initial marketing promoting a comfortable no-frills service with a Spanish theme and onboard menus celebrating the regions of the country. The service started on 29th April with a crossing time on the 550-nautical-mile route of 26 hours. The *Connemara's* schedule also included a weekly round trip from Cork to Roscoff. In the year when Brittany Ferries celebrated the fortieth anniversary of sailings to both Ireland and Spain, the Irish connection was going from strength to strength, with 2017 registering a four per cent increase in passengers to 87,000 on the back of a three per cent increase in 2016, so the year-round weekly sailing of the *Connemara* from Cork to Roscoff was a welcome addition to the weekly seasonal 14-hour crossing of the *Pont-Aven*.

More positive news came with confirmation of the charter of a second new generation 'E-Flexer' cruise-ferries from Stena RoRo to serve the Spanish routes. Both vessels now on order were designed to be LNG-ready and promised a combination of luxury and Spanish style. As with the rest of the E-Flexer fleet, the vessels were to be built at the AVIC International Weihai shipyard in China. The twin ships outwardly would have the same dimensions and shape, but with interiors designed by Spanish interior designers to give each vessel a unique stylish, modern feel, evoking the golden coasts, verdant landscapes, and vibrant towns of España Verde (Green Spain) on the northern coastline. Three spacious passenger decks would incorporate boutiques, cafés, a restaurant, bars, and an exclusive club lounge. Measuring 42,400-gt and 215 metres long, the vessels would include 300 en-suite cabins and cater for around 1,000 passengers with deck space for almost two miles of freight vehicles apiece. The new vessels would be the longest in Brittany Ferries' fleet, enabling the Company to operate sister ships in the fleet for the first time. There were plans for both vessels to be based in Portsmouth.

The names *Galicia* and *Salamanca* were chosen for the vessels arriving in November 2021 and 2022 respectively, following a competition amongst Brittany Ferries' staff. The arrival of the *Galicia* would enable the *Baie de Seine* to be returned to her owners DFDS; the *Salamanca* would replace the *Cap Finistère*. These two new additions, added to the existing order for the *Honfleur*, spearheaded a wide-ranging, five-year fleet-renewal and modernisation programme worth around £400m. In the meantime, project Bretagne II continued as an important and parallel part of the fleet renewal strategy.

The first direct ferry sailing from Ireland to Spain took place on 10th May 2018 when the *Connemara* left Cork

The *Connemara* leaves Le Havre following her overhaul at the port. *(Pascal Bredel)*

for Santander with 200 passengers and 80 vehicles onboard. The run up to this departure was tortuous. The *Asterion* finished Adriatic service at Patras on 8th April, leaving just three weeks for refit and repositioning for the planned first voyage, but the condition of the vessel was sufficiently poor to require additional work, and her inaugural sailing was put back until 6th May from Santander. This was subsequently cancelled to enable the Irish Authorities to inspect the *Connemara;* she sailed light for Cork arriving there on 7th May. Her first departure was therefore the weekly sailing to France, but this sailed to Brest rather than Roscoff to avoid demonstrations in the port planned by the French Trade Union CDFT, disputing the operation of a Cypriot-registered ship with a non-French crew.

The *Connemara* was repainted in a hybrid Brittany Ferries livery, keeping her red lower hull with white upper works; a Brittany Ferries logo was placed on the hull and the funnel repainted into fleet livery. Although marketed under the Économie brand, this did not feature in the livery, unlike her Économie consorts *Étretat* and *Bai de Seine*. Brittany Ferries publicised ambitious plans to carry 20,000 freight units and 40,000 passengers on the new service during the first year of operation, despite there being only two sailings per week in each direction and a highly seasonal passenger business.

The introduction of the *Connemara* contributed to a rise in Company-wide passenger traffic of two per cent over the 2018 summer season compared with 2017. Unsurprisingly the strongest performance came from the Cork-Roscoff route on which passenger traffic grew by nine per cent. The *Connemara* also contributed to a 12 per cent rise on long-haul routes operating between the UK, Spain, and Ireland. The most popular route, Portsmouth-Caen, which carries around 30 per cent of passengers, increased by two per cent. Only Plymouth-Roscoff (down one per cent) and Cherbourg-Portsmouth (down nine per cent) reported a drop in numbers, the latter decline reflecting a shorter season for the Company's summer operation of the high-speed craft, *Normandie Express*.

The *Honfleur* was launched at midday on 14th December 2018, as hundreds lined the quaysides to see the completed hull slide down into the Flensburg Fjord. Some 118 steel hull sections had been welded together on the slipway to create the 10,000 tonne six-storey ship since the cutting of the first steel in March and the laying of the keel in August. The completed hull contained the ship's main machinery, including its LNG-electric propulsion system. Two giant superstructures 'mega blocks' remained to be hoisted into position by giant cranes; at this time these were en route by barge from the shipyards in Poland where they had been built.

As these positive developments unfolded, cross-Channel operators began to draw attention to the consequences of a 'no-deal' Brexit and the impact on free movement of an emerging requirement for enhanced customs checks at ports. The UK government sought to spread the risk by seeking contracts to guarantee continuity of freight capacity on routes away from likely congestion at Dover but drew ridicule by seeking to secure a contract with Seaborne, a company with no track record in shipping; Dover, which accounted for 17 percent of the U.K.'s trade in goods, pointed out the difficulties of establishing such alternative routes at short notice. With continued concerns over Brexit at Portsmouth, and to a lesser extent at Poole and Plymouth, there was great uncertainty for Brittany Ferries and the port operators, with a Brexit deadline of 29th March 2019 fast approaching. Portsmouth City council sought to use part of the M275 as a lorry park in the event of a 'hard' Brexit. Meanwhile, the uncertainty surrounding validity of pet travel, health insurance, and driving licences discouraged British holidaymakers from booking their summer 2019 ferry crossings, and Brittany Ferries advance bookings were up to five per cent down on 2018 levels.

In the freight sector, the UK Department of Transport (DfT) sought clarification on spare freight capacity on routes west of Calais. Brittany Ferries looked at increasing the frequency of services into Cherbourg and Le Havre but warned that every vehicle carrying refrigerated goods, food and other natural products would still face possible inspection upon arrival in France. Around one third of the 210,000 freight units carried by Brittany Ferries annually would be affected. The infrastructure needed for this operation necessitated the provision of large warehouses which did not exist in Roscoff, St Malo or Cherbourg, nor was it possible that they could be constructed by March 2019.

Trading uncertainty began to impact Brittany Ferries' cash flow. With the *Honfleur* scheduled to join the flagship Portsmouth-Caen route in 2019, and two further ships following as part of the €450m investment plan by 2022, this could not have happened at a worse time.

Eventually a contract was agreed with the DfT to change 2019 sailing schedules to offer capacity for freight traffic displaced from potential Brexit-related congestion on the short sea routes. 19 return-sailings were added each week to the Plymouth-Roscoff, Poole-Cherbourg and Portsmouth-Le Havre routes. These additional rotations created a 50 per cent increase in freight capacity on the three routes from 29th March 2019, and a 30 per cent increase overall on the western Channel.

The Company was continuing to take a long-term view of business prospects and announced the signing of an agreement with Stena RoRo for the charter of a third E-Flexer vessel to join the fleet on the Spanish routes from 2023. The LNG-powered vessel would

The **_Barfleur_** captured leaving Portsmouth whilst operating on the Caen link. _(Darren Holdaway)_

The **_Pont-Aven_** laid up at Le Havre as she waits to enter service for another summer season. _(Pascal Bredel)_

match her two sisters in outward configuration and would again be fitted out in distinctive Spanish style. The charter agreement included a future option to purchase the vessel, which was to be named *Santoña*. This positive news was overshadowed by delays to delivery of the *Honfleur*, with her handover put back until autumn 2019, thereby missing the summer season.

The *Connemara's* twice-weekly Cork-Santander no-frills 'Économie' route, coupled with the weekly Cork-Roscoff crossing continued for 2019, despite suggestions that freight loadings on the Spanish link had been below expectations. Brexit uncertainty prompted a rapidly changing outlook, and the Company was clear from the outset that this route would take time to develop. Cork-Roscoff passenger figures fared a little better, increasing by ten per cent, although the introduction of the weekly crossing had resulted in around a 20 per cent increase in passenger capacity over the existing weekly seasonal *Pont-Aven* sailing on the route. The winter schedule of the *Connemara* was modified, with the Roscoff sailing dropped from November 2018 until the following spring. With a crew predominantly comprising of EU rather than French nationals, the call in Roscoff was not needed for crew changeover, and stores and supplies were trucked down to Santander to service the vessel during the layovers each Wednesday and Thursday. The summer 2019 schedule reinstated the weekly Roscoff sailing from 4th March until the end of October, on a similar basis to 2018.

Just before 04:00 on 29th April, the crew on *Pont-Aven* were alerted to a fire in the ship's engine room during a crossing from Plymouth to Santander. The vessel was approximately 100 nautical miles south of Brest with 766 passengers and 142 crew on board. The fire was quickly extinguished, there were no injuries, but the *Pont-Aven* was diverted to Brest, arriving at around 15:00. All traffic disembarked, and Brittany Ferries' technical teams commenced a full investigation into the incident. Some traffic transferred to Portsmouth-Spain sailings, but the *Armorique* switched to cover Friday and Saturday sailings on the Roscoff-Cork route, despite her limited cabin capacity. The Plymouth-Roscoff schedule faced a forced re-scheduled and was cancelled at weekends. The *Pont-Aven* returned after her repair in Brest with only three of four engines in operation; this brought a reduction in service speed, forcing all her Spanish sailings to be concentrated on Plymouth for the rest of the year.

The *Pont-Aven* re-entered service on 13th May but then experienced hydraulic problems with one of her

A powerful view of the *Mont St Michel* leaving Portsmouth for Caen in March 2021. *(Darren Holdaway)*

two steering gear systems whilst berthing at Roscoff; this forced her to return to Brest for further repairs that kept her out of service until 14th June. Disruption to the complex Portsmouth-Santander-Plymouth-Roscoff-Cork schedule of the *Pont-Aven* saw the Plymouth-Santander, Roscoff-Cork routes, and some weekend sailings between Plymouth and Roscoff cancelled in consequence. The *Armorique* covered several of the Cork sailings, making her first ever visit to the city. However, the weekend three-night Cork-Santander round trip of the *Connemara* was cancelled for three weekends from the late May Bank Holiday to allow the vessel to make two round back-to-back trips between Cork and Roscoff, with Santander traffic routed via road through France.

The chartered *Bore Bay* arrived at Poole on 27th August to cover the Bilbao freight service whilst exhaust scrubbers were fitted to the regular vessel *MN Pelican*. The *Bore Bay* had a slightly smaller capacity than the *MN Pelican* but with berths for 12 drivers. The *MN Pelican* returned to service at the end 2019.

Two key milestones in the €550m fleet renewal programme were celebrated on 10th September. Shipyard workers and Company teams gathered at the AVIC Weihai shipyard in Shandong, China, to celebrate the launch of *Galicia*, and the start of building work on for sister ship *Salamanca*. The 215m-long hull of the *Galicia* was floated out at a traditional Chinese ship-launching ceremony. Then, alongside in the building dock, the first steel was cut for the *Salamanca*, marking the beginning of the ship's construction. The *Galicia* was launched with Portsmouth as her port of registry, but she was due to be re-registered under the French flag prior to her entry into service. The *Galicia* was being built fitted with funnel exhaust gas cleaning systems, whilst sisters *Salamanca* and *Santoña* were to incorporate LNG power plants. The series of three ships will be managed by Northern Marine, part of the Stena Group.

Meanwhile, the Company's very first LNG-powered ship *Honfleur* was still under construction in Flensburg, Germany with her entry into service on the Portsmouth-Caen route now put back until spring 2020.

The 2019 results saw a drop in both passenger and freight volumes, although turnover increased by about 5.5% to €469m. Brittany Ferries President Jean-Marc Roué told shareholders that tourism remained an important part of the company's DNA, as the company played a key role in the economic and tourist development of the regions it directly or indirectly served. He observed that 857,000 of its travellers spent over €586m in France, staying a total of 8.7 million nights in French hotels, lodges, campsites, and holiday homes. Brittany Ferries operated a fleet of 13 ferries in 2019, carrying 2.49m passengers, a 4.9% drop on 2018. The number of tourist vehicles shrank by 5% to 865,989. A total of 201,554 freight vehicles were transported, a 1.9% decrease on 2018. The Brexit process was blamed, with uncertainty responsible for lower volumes, as three successive Brexit-date postponements influenced travel behaviour of British customers in 2019. In fiscal year 2018, Brittany Ferries had posted an €8m profit. For the fiscal year 2019, Brittany Ferries only reported its turnover figure.

The freight vessel *AF Michela* (previously the *Stena Egeria*) was chartered from Stena Ro-Ro to become the third of its kind to join the Brittany Ferries fleet, alongside the *Étretat* and *Connemara*. The twelve-month charter commenced in October 2019. The chartered Visentini-class vessel was renamed the *Kerry*, continuing the Irish-themed nomenclature series. The *Kerry* took up the Cork-Santander link from 31st October, her twelve-month charter enabled her to cover the Cork operations to France and Spain. Meanwhile, the *Connemara* was re-registered under the French flag on 6th November, bringing the number of French-registered vessels in the Brittany Ferries fleet to eleven and creating some 111 jobs for French seafarers.

Information Area on the *Barfleur*. *(Darren Holdaway)*

Turquoise self-service restaurant on the *Barfleur*. *(Darren Holdaway)*

The 2020's - A difficult start

The *Bretagne* completed her season on the St Malo route on 3rd November 2019, with her place taken by the *Pont-Aven* until the end of the year. The *Bretagne* was then scheduled to return to cover the roster on the link for the remainder of 2020. The *Connemara* covered for the refit of the *Barfleur* on Poole-Cherbourg service at the end of 2019, whilst the Plymouth-Roscoff route was maintained by the *Armorique* until 5th January. The route re-opened on 11th February, after the *Armorique* spent time covering the Caen service.

The *Pont-Aven* was taken out of service to undergo a major refit at Gdansk from 3rd January to 17th March 2020, that included a complete replacement of the engine damaged by the fire in 2019; the work involved a hole being cut into the side of the hull to allow the engine to be removed and inserted. This prompted an interesting period of ship deployment, as the fleet operating on different routes from normal. On the Caen link, the *Armorique* again covered the refits of the *Mont St Michel* and *Normandie*. The *Connemara* took up station on the Portsmouth-Le Havre service with the *Étretat*, offering two round sailings a day throughout the winter. Meanwhile the *Baie de Seine* offered an additional weekly sailing to allow for a crew change at the French port. The *Baie de Seine* made her final sailing on the Le Havre link on 12th March, prior to the end of her charter with the Company for whom she had operated since 2015.

On the Spanish operations, the Portsmouth-Santander link was covered by the *Baie de Seine* and *Connemara*, whilst the *Cap Finistère* went for her refit. The *Connemara* operated on the Spanish link from mid-March in place of the *Baie de Seine*. The Bilbao link closed from 30th October until 27th November, and thereafter was maintained by *Cap Finistère* and *Baie de Seine* until the end of her charter. The *Connemara* replaced the chartered DFDS ship on the link from March. On the Irish link, the *Pont-Aven* closed the Roscoff-Cork service on 2 November until reopening again on 21st March 2020.

Brittany Ferries embarked on a series of 'dry runs' to prepare for the possible consequences of a no-deal Brexit on both sides of the Channel on 11th September, involving lorries on the overnight Portsmouth-Caen service. Information about freight vehicles boarding vessels in the UK was sent electronically to French customs officers, who divided vehicles into a green channel for those with advance clearance, and orange for those requiring inspection upon arrival in France. Drivers were informed of their vehicle's status by onboard information screens. On arrival in France, lorries in the green channel bypassed customs controls as they exit the port. Some 15 rehearsals are planned up until mid-October.

The *Cap Finistère* became the longest ferry ever to operate on the Portsmouth-Le Havre route when she replaced the *Étretat* on the link, whilst she went to Poland for annual overhaul; the *Cap Finistère* operated one round trip a week on Le Havre service during her absence.

There was still great uncertainty about the entry into service date of the *Honfleur*, with her planned introduction put back until 9th September 2020. More positively, work on three 'E Flexer' ships continued at a rapid rate, with the *Galicia* due to enter service in the late Autumn 2020.

As hauliers and transport operators sought ways to reduce greenhouse gas emissions and other pollutants, Brittany Ferries outlined plans to diversify its operations and introduce an intermodal transport service for unaccompanied goods-trailers, using dedicated trains on the SNCF railway network to the French-Atlantic coast. The Company had been conducting extensive feasibility studies for a road-rail service between Cherbourg and the Bayonne/Mougeuerre areas of France since 2018. The planned service complemented the existing UK-Spain 'Motorway of the Sea' concept by switching mode for goods travelling overland between the UK and the Iberian Peninsula from road to rail. The project also met increasing demand for a 'modal shift' from those freight customers seeking to lower emissions compared with overland transport by road to and from the port, and reduced dependence on road drivers.

The rail service could accommodate a wide range of trailer traffic, including those loaded by cranes and 'swap body' vehicles. The project envisaged harnessing the 'Lohr', pivot-based, loading system, with the installation of fixed stations at ground level. This allows the chassis of rail vehicles to be turned by around 45 degrees, allowing loading, and unloading of standard road semi-trailers. Railway stations would need to be equipped with electrical, hydraulic and pneumatics to control the movement of trailers.

The **Bretagne** arrives at Portsmouth on her early morning seasonal overnight sailing from St Malo. For the majority of the year the **Bretagne** normally has operated overnight from Portsmouth to St Malo and on daylight schedules from St Malo to the UK. *(Darren Holdaway)*

The project anticipated future EU regulatory challenges in reducing transport emissions, especially in relation to maritime transport. It presented an attractive, environmentally friendly service for both shippers and hauliers, reducing road congestion, the number of potential accidents, and wear and tear on road infrastructure. The project also had significant advantages for Brittany Ferries, allowing the Company to facilitate a potential increase in the volume of unaccompanied freight traffic as a proportion of its overall freight business. At the start of the decade, this stood at 20% of freight business across all routes, and 25% on the direct routes between the UK and Spain. Although port handling costs and turnround times would need to incorporate the movement of trailers on and off the fleet, the absence of a tractor unit on each trailer on board the vessel halves the weight of each vehicle carried on board and reduces garage space requirements by some 20 per cent. The arrival of new ships to the fleet with enhanced garage space gave plentiful opportunities to expand the service.

The chartered DFDS vessel *Baie de Seine* completed the 17:15 sailing from Santander to Portsmouth on 11th March, and after her arrival at Portsmouth undertook a 23:00 departure to Le Havre on 12th March, before de-storing ready to be handed back to her Danish owners. She sailed to Poland three days later for a major overhaul. Her roster was then covered by the *Connemara*, ahead of the arrival of the *Galicia*, the first of the 'E Flexer' ships to be delivered from China in early autumn 2020.

Brittany Ferries' twice weekly 'Économie' sailings, operated by the *Kerry* between Cork and Santander, and the seasonal weekly sailing from Cork to Roscoff, moved

The early morning sun catches the **Barfleur** as she turns off Brownsea Castle en route for Sandbanks and the open sea to Cherbourg. *(Kevin Mitchell)*

The **Honfleur** under construction in Flensburg. Brittany Ferries terminated the contract for the ship with the FSG shipyard on 17th June 2020. *(FSG Shipyard)*

Sad times for the world and for Brittany Ferries. The view shows the ***Bretagne***, ***Normandie Express*** and ***Pont-Aven*** laid up at Le Havre during the pandemic in 2020. *(Pascal Bredel)*

The *Normandie Express* laid up at Darse de l'Ocean, Le Havre in 2022. *(Pascal Bredel)*

Another vessel laid-up during the pandemic in 2020 was the chartered *Connemara*. *(Pascal Bredel)*

to Rosslare from 28th February, with the Spanish destination terminal switching to Bilbao. This move followed extensive consultation with freight customers, who expressed a preference for using both Rosslare and Bilbao, as these ports had significantly better onward road connections. However, the seasonal weekly connection between Cork and Roscoff would continue to be provided by the *Pont-Aven* from Cork.

Brittany Ferries opened another new route between Roscoff and Rosslare on 23rd March, following the move of the passenger/freight service between Ireland and Spain from Cork in late February.

Brittany Ferries further expanded their activity by completing the purchase of Condor and their Channel Island operations, as a minority partner with the Columbia Threadneedle European Sustainable Infrastructure Fund, on 9th March 2020. The partners said they were "looking forward to working with management, employees and the Channel Islands". The Condor operation had substantial synergies with the rest of Brittany Ferries' operations, with the main UK passenger base in Poole, freight operations at Portsmouth, and important routes from Guernsey and Jersey to St Malo.

All the Company's plans for 2020 were put into disarray when the Covid-19 pandemic began to spread widely in Europe in March 2020. As the impact of the virus became clearer, European countries moved into domestic 'lockdown' conditions, with severe restrictions on international movement. This led to a rapid shutdown of national economies and a cessation of passenger travel. The consequences were unprecedented in peacetime.

The Spanish services were the first of the Company's

to close, with the *Connemara* undertaking her last sailing back to the UK on 19th March 2020 and *Cap Finistère* carrying out the last passenger sailing from Santander on 21st March. There was still demand for freight services, particularly for foodstuffs, so the *Cap Finistère* continued to sail on a freight-only operation to Spain, alongside the *Pelican* from Poole and the *Kerry* which continued to serve Spain from Ireland. The sailing schedules for the *Pont-Aven*, which was due to re-enter service on 17th March following her extensive refit period in Poland, were quickly cancelled, so after sailing to Roscoff to take on stores she continued to Le Havre and was laid-up in the port.

On the French routes, the *Étretat* was withdrawn from service on 17th March. The *Normandie* completed her final sailing on the Portsmouth-Caen service on the same day, whilst the *Mont St Michel* continued her normal schedule on the Portsmouth-Caen link but operating in freight-only mode. The *Connemara* was deployed on a new freight-only Portsmouth-Cherbourg service from 20th March. The *Bretagne* undertook the final sailing from St Malo on 17th March with the 20:30 departure to Portsmouth, the day before the *Barfleur* closed the Poole-Cherbourg link. The Plymouth-Roscoff route was forced to close on 18th March. Henceforth, all freight drivers travelling on the Company's fleet during the lock down period were required to take their own food, as all catering and shop facilities on board were closed.

The *Kerry's* twice-weekly Rosslare-Bilbao 'Économie' service, which had only begun on 28th February in place of the vessel's previous Cork-Santander service, was placed into freight-only mode, but the weekly round-trip from Rosslare to Roscoff was suspended before it began, with the *Kerry* laying over the equivalent period in Rosslare. With France effectively closed off to outside visitors, the *Pont-Aven's* seasonal weekly connection between Cork and Roscoff was also suspended. Although these changes were initially planned to continue until late April, the pandemic forced these arrangements to continue into June.

Most of the fleet was now out of service. The *Armorique* was sent to lay-up in Cherbourg, the *Barfleur* in the city of Caen, and the *Pont-Aven, Normandie, Normandie Express, Étretat,* and *Bretagne* were laid up in the inner basin of Darse de 'l'Ocean at Le Havre.

With much of European industry, including shipyards, in continued closure, there was little prospect of the *Honfleur* being delivered soon, even to her new much-delayed timescales. The vessel had been under construction in Flensburg since 2017, and was originally scheduled to enter service in June 2019, but delivery was postponed several times due to the persistent financial problems encountered by FSG. The Company's backers lost confidence in FSG's ability to complete the vessel within a reasonable period. Brittany Ferries and Somanor SAS (the semi-public company bringing together the Normandy Region, and the Calvados and Manche Départements), confirmed the termination of the build contract for the *Honfleur* with the FSG shipyard on 17th June 2020.

This decision still left the Company committed to three new E-Flexer vessels for the Spanish operations over next three years despite the pandemic. Meanwhile, the FSG yard confirmed their commitment to complete the *Honfleur*.

The ongoing travel restrictions left Brittany Ferries in a difficult trading position. The Company was heavily dependent on the passenger market, and it was suffering heavily from the Covid-19 crisis. Prospects for normal summer traffic in 2020 gradually receded as the year progressed.

Both Spain and France re-opened their borders to tourist visitors from late June. The *Mont St Michael* re-opened passenger sailings between Portsmouth and Caen on 29th June, with the *Cap Finistère* re-commencing passenger operations to Santander and the *Armorique* opening the Plymouth-Roscoff route on the same day. The *Pont- Aven* commenced her usual weekly roster on 30th June with sailings to Santander, Plymouth, Roscoff and Cork. Meanwhile, the *Connemara* opened the Portsmouth-Cherbourg and Portsmouth-Le Havre services from 10th July and the *Normandie* re-entered service on the Portsmouth-Caen link from 12th July, followed by the *Bretagne* five days later on the Portsmouth-St Malo route. However, the Company suspended the *Étretat, Barfleur,* and *Normandie Express* from operations for the remainder of 2020, so there were to be no passenger services from Poole to Cherbourg following the *Barfleur's* withdrawal.

Passenger operations restarted from Ireland in late June. The *Kerry* finally commenced the seasonal weekly Rosslare-Roscoff 'Économie' service on 29th June, which had been suspended prior to its planned 23rd March start, and the vessel's twice-weekly Rosslare-Bilbao sailings were re-opened to passengers. The weekly Cork-Roscoff sailing of the *Pont-Aven* was also reinstated, with the vessel re-entering service on 3rd July after her period of lay-up in Le Havre.

With the gradual resumption of passenger services, Brittany Ferries published a 12-point guide as part of a campaign called 'Together & Protected', to reassure passengers as to the safety of its operations. Passengers and crew were required to wear masks in public areas whilst on board the ships and in the port areas. In addition, all ships maintained the use of virucidal products throughout the vessel, with enhanced regular cleaning programmes on all sailings. Passenger numbers were scaled back to allow sensible social distancing rules to be enforced on board; boarding and disembarkation timings were also staggered to avoid queues on the stairs and car decks, and check-in times were extended to close 90 minutes before departure. A cabin or reserved seating became compulsory on sailings. Catering operations also underwent change, with the withdrawal of on-board buffets, replaced by meals ordered and served to passengers. There were significant operational hurdles in handling foot passengers and cyclists amidst all these changes, so bookings for these traffics were not accepted for the remainder of 2020.

The resumption of services allowed passengers to begin booking their summer holidays in France and Spain and there were prospects of summer revenues. But there were sharp rises in the number of Covid-19 cases in France, Spain, and the UK as the summer progressed, and from 27th July the UK government mandated that all passengers returning from Spain would be required to self-isolate for 14 days; quarantine requirements were then placed on passengers returning from France to the UK from 15th August. These short notice changes immediately dampened down demand.

Brittany Ferries lobbied the French government at the highest levels to avoid the implementation of reciprocal quarantine measures, claiming that, despite new quarantine restrictions, many passengers were making an informed decision and still taking holidays. The Company planned to continue to serve both French and Spanish destinations despite these new UK restrictions. But there was an immediate impact on business. Some 35,000 passengers either cancelled or delayed their travel plans in the first weekend after the quarantine announcement. The situation was untenable. Four days after the UK self-isolating rules were introduced, Brittany Ferries was forced to announce major changes to planned scheduled services from the end of August 2020, also noting that forward demand for autumn sailings was extremely weak.

The *Armorique* was laid up from the Plymouth-Roscoff service from 31st August, with her place taken by the *Pont-Aven* offering three return trips per week on the route in addition to one return sailing from Plymouth to Santander and one each week from Roscoff to Cork until 25th October. The *Bretagne* was laid up from 7th September and the *Étretat* was also withdrawn from service. It was planned that the *Connemara* would continue to operate the Cherbourg and Le Havre rotations from Portsmouth but no longer serve Spain.

There was hope that this new strategy would enable the Company to continue to offer a credible service through the autumn. But Covid-19 cases in the UK, France, and Spain continued to rise and traffic prospects became increasingly bleak. The need quickly emerged for the implementation of more schedule changes to significantly reduce costs and help maintain the trajectory of the Company's five-year recovery plan. The most significant immediate change became the withdrawal of the *Connemara* from 7th September, resulting in the closure of both the Portsmouth-Cherbourg and Portsmouth- Le Havre routes. The *Normandie* and *Mont St Michel* continued their three daily departures on the Portsmouth-Caen service,

The *Galicia* is floated out from her construction dock on 10th September 2019. *(Brittany Ferries)*

with plans for the *Armorique* running in freight-only mode to cover each ship's technical overhaul during November and December respectively. The *Cap Finistère* remained in operation on the Bilbao and Santander routes until late November, before being withdrawn from service for two months for an extensive refit and overhaul, with a planned return to service on 27th January 2021. The *Pont-Aven* maintained the Santander, Roscoff and Cork links from Plymouth until 25th October, and then transferred to Portsmouth to operate with the *Cap Finistère* until 1st December; thereafter the new *Galicia* covered the Santander service only. The *Kerry* and *Pelican* remained in service on the Rosslare-Bilbao and Poole-Bilbao routes as planned. By mid-September, the *Connemara, Bretagne, Armorique, Étretat,* and *Normandie Express* were all laid up in Le Havre by the pandemic, and the *Barfleur* remained laid up in Caen.

Christophe Mathieu starkly noted that "we carried virtually no passenger traffic between the months of April and June, as the Covid-19 crisis hit. When we resumed, we had hoped to salvage 350,000 passengers from a summer season that would usually achieve more than double that number. The reality however is that we are unlikely to reach 200,000. Passenger traffic accounts for around 75% of our income, so our bottom line has been hit hard. It's why we must continue to take decisive action to reduce our costs to get us through the worst of this unprecedented crisis. Over the weekend of 30 August, we had capacity for 5,400 passengers and we ended up carrying 2,300. To give you an idea, last year, for the same weekend, we carried 13,400 passengers. In other words, we were looking at a season around 40% down, with the quarantine announcement, the season will end with at least a halving of bookings."

With much of the Company's potential 2020 revenue lost and little prospect of any immediate improvement, Brittany Ferries turned to the French government for help, stating that the UK's imposition of quarantine restrictions in August during the peak season had brought the company to its knees. French Prime Minister Jean Castex responded on 15th September, by announcing help for French ferry companies through the reimbursement of payroll taxes. Brittany Ferries would receive €15m from a national budget of €30m. On the same day, the Presidents of the Brittany and Normandy regions promised a further €85m in support to the Company. Chairman Jean-Marc Roué thanked the two regional presidents, saying that, "They seem to be the only ones who understand the importance of the cross-Channel ferry traffic. They have been the only ones to effectively help the French seafarer and the few companies that still hire them."

Meanwhile, despite the worldwide pandemic, the Company's new E-Flexer *Galicia* was nearing completion at the Jinling Shipyard in Weihai, China, with her successful sea trials taking place in late August and September. The *Galicia* was handed over in the early hours of 3rd September to Per Westling, Stena RoRo's managing director, whilst he was seated in his Gothenburg office with Christophe Mathieu.

The *Galicia* left Qingdao, China on 15th September en route to Europe via Singapore. Brittany Ferries hired a crew from Stena AB subsidiary Northern Marine to bring *Galicia* to her new home. On the 10,000-mile voyage to Europe, she was still registered under the British flag in Portsmouth but was set to be re-registered in Morlaix once the charter papers between

The *Kerry* pictured arriving at Roscoff. *(Brittany Ferries)*

The *Armorique* at Rosslare during February 2021. *(Ferry Publications Library)*

Stena RoRo and Brittany Ferries were completed on her arrival in France. She carried out berthing trials in Portsmouth, Cherbourg, Bilbao, Santander, Brest, Plymouth and Le Havre during October and November, and went into drydock at the Astander shipyard in Santander in the middle of this programme of scheduled port visits.

The *Galicia* was bespoke designed for the Spanish market, with a décor inspired by the Spanish region from which she takes her name, the first time that Brittany Ferries designed and decorated a ship around a

Spanish theme. She was also the first fleet vessel to feature an airline-style premium lounge, with drinks and snacks included in the entrance charge. Other facilities included a beach-themed Azul restaurant, the town-square-inspired Plaza Mayor bar, and a Taberna de Tapas. One dinner and a continental breakfast were to be included in the fare for all passengers on UK-Spain sailings. The *Galicia* was designed to produce significantly lower levels of emissions relative to ships of a similar size and was equipped with two in-line exhaust gas scrubbers. She brought capacity for 3,100 freight lane-metres and 1,015 passengers. The deckhouses on decks 7 and 8 were extended further than the standard E-Flexer design to adapt the vessel for its overnight services and deliver capacity of 1,233 beds in 343 passenger cabins.

Although the Company was navigating a difficult, turbulent summer, there was a commercial need to develop and publish the 2021 schedule of sailings. In a new development the seasonal Cork-Roscoff route was to be increased to two return crossings each week by the *Armorique,* offering the additional sailing in between her Plymouth-Roscoff roster. The season's first sailing of the *Armorique* was scheduled for 23rd March with the *Pont-Aven* following on 26th March. The Rosslare-Bilbao service was to be continued over the winter, but industrial action at Bilbao diverted the Rosslare service to Santander during the final couple of weeks of operation of the *Kerry* before she returned to Stena RoRo on completion of her charter. The *Kerry* stood down in Santander on 4th November, with her crew switching to the *Connemara* that took over the link on 8th November. The *Connemara* was reflagged from the French Tricolour back to the Cypriot flag for her second spell on the Ireland-Spain link, continuing to serve Santander as the period of industrial action continued through into December. The switch to the *Connemara* was designed to increase competition for Stena Line's Rosslare-Cherbourg link operated by near Visentini sister the *Stena Horizon,* and with the *Armorique* undertaking a new weekly Roscoff-Cork return crossing, Brittany Ferries' Ireland-France crossings increased from two to three.

Meanwhile, Brittany Ferries won another of the 'post-Brexit' freight subsidy contracts from the UK DfT on 13th October to guarantee space on services connecting Portsmouth with Le Havre and Poole with Cherbourg from January 2021.

The 215m 41,000-gt vessel *Galicia* made her first commercial arrival into Portsmouth at 19:00 on 3rd December 2020, greeted by an impressive firework display. Some 500 passengers and freight drivers were on board, along with 240 cars and 100 lorries, having made the 27-hour crossing from Santander. But her arrival was overshadowed by another sequence of severe international Covid-19 lockdowns.

Although constructed in China, the E-Flexer is a European design created by Finnish naval architect Deltamarin in conjunction with Stena RoRo. The *Galicia's* E-Flexer design has large panoramic windows in the passenger areas and a central atrium feature that makes the vessel feel light and airy. There are ten decks with the uppermost being the Sun Deck and passenger areas concentrated on decks 7, 8 and 9. The 343 cabins are found across all three passenger decks at the aft end, with four grades of cabin provided. On Deck 7 is the Information desk, a foyer and the open information lounge with a staircase leading upwards to the Plaza Mayor Bar atrium on Deck 8. Access is available from the information area to sheltered side promenades with heated dog kennels and a pet exercise area. A walking passage runs along the port side with open seating, and two boutique shops on the starboard side. The 325 seat Restaurant Azul occupies the full width of *Galicia* and features large panoramic windows with views over the bow. Deck 8 features the 148-seat C-Club Lounge, again with views over the bow. Aft of this lie two seating areas and the 174-seat Taberna de Tapas restaurant. The Plaza Mayor Bar spans the full width of the atrium; aft of this can be found further small lounges. The vessel with adorned with art that supports the Camino de Santiago theme, with works curated by artist Kimberley Poppe. With three children's play areas, an outside gym, an exhibition on La Casa de Las Meninas, and a Sea Travel exhibition, the Galicia redefined the Spanish crossing experience.

Passenger operations were once again reduced to the minimum. The only the passenger vessels in operation during December 2020 were the *Normandie, Connemara,* and *Galicia.* The *Cap Finistère* was set to cover the *Connemara* on the Rosslare-Bilbao link for four weeks from 22nd January 2021. The *Normandie* was laid up from 4th January 2021 leaving the *Mont St Michel* to cover the Caen link alone until late March. This remained the status-quo until the *Cap Finistère* re-entered operations on the Bilbao and Santander services.

The charter of the *Stena Baltica* to Stena Line concluded in December and she was renamed *Cotentin* again at Le Havre whilst undergoing her refit. The Finnish-built ship re-entered service with Brittany Ferries on the Poole-Cherbourg service on 1st January 2021, remaining on the Poole link until 4th April 2021, when the *Barfleur* took up operations again. The *Cotentin* then transferred to operate the Portsmouth-Le Havre service until the end of 2021.

Unsurprisingly, passenger numbers fell to less than a third of normal levels in 2020, a year dominated by Covid-19 and on-going Brexit concerns. The freight business fared slightly better, with figures down by 20%. Turnover halved, as lockdown restrictions forced passengers to stay at home. The Company observed that the value of Sterling against the Euro had plummeted directly after the 2016 vote and, since then, the Company

The *Étretat* leaves Le Havre at the end of her charter to Brittany Ferries. On her return to Stena RoRo she was renamed the ***Stena Livia***. *(Pascal Bredel)*

Following the ending of her charter to Stena Line the ***Cotentin*** was sent for a major overhaul. She is pictured here arriving at Le Havre following her overhaul prior to entering service between Poole and Cherbourg. *(Pascal Bredel)*

GALICIA

The *Galicia* undergoing berthing trials at Le Havre. *(Pascal Bredel)*

Galicia

Above: **The *Galicia* pictured during her first visit to Roscoff.** *(Brittany Ferries)*

Top right: **Father Christian Bernard blesses *Galicia*.** *(Brittany Ferries)*

Bottom right: **Club Class Lounge on the *Galicia*.** *(Brittany Ferries)*

Below: **Information Lounge - *Galicia*.** *(Brittany Ferries)*

Above: **Azul Restaurant - *Galicia.*** *(Brittany Ferries)*

Left: **Plaza Mayor Bar - *Galicia.*** *(Brittany Ferries)*

Bottom left: **Tapas Tavern - *Galicia.*** *(Brittany Ferries)*

Below: **De Luxe Cabin - *Galicia.*** *(Brittany Ferries)*

Brittany Ferries had no sister ships in their fleet until the arrival of the *Galicia*. By 2023 they will have three 'E Flexer' vessels, with two similar sisters to follow by 2025. *(Darren Holdaway)*

The *Galicia* berthing at Plymouth on her first visit to the Devon port. *(Brittany Ferries)*

had lost €115m in potential income on a balance sheet where most revenue was still generated in Sterling and most Costs incurred in Euros. Brexit concerns were also affecting demand. Three potential dates for the UK's departure from the EU in 2019 had created almost continuous uncertainty and anxiety in the marketplace, resulting in an ongoing fall in passenger numbers

Brittany Ferries gradually extended their suspension of passenger services across the winter. Five ships (the *Barfleur, Bretagne, Cap Finistère, Pont-Aven* and *Étretat* – the latter shortly due to handed back to Stena RoRo) were laid-up in Le Havre and Cherbourg. Normal passenger operations were initially due to resume in late March, but revised plans gradually ushered these dates backwards. Meanwhile, the *Armorique* (Cork-Roscoff freight service), *Connemara* (Rosslare-Cherbourg, Rosslare-Bilbao), *Cotentin* (Poole-Cherbourg until 2nd April), *Galicia* (Portsmouth-Santander, Portsmouth-Cherbourg) and *Normandie* and *Mont St Michel* (Portsmouth-Caen) continued to operate as scheduled to accommodate essential passenger travel requirements and allow freight traffic to flow freely.

The austere financial position that these shutdowns generated prompted the formulation of a new five-year plan to span the period during which the Company was expected to pay back the loans received to bridge their bleakest period in decades. The four pillars of the plan were: -

Energy transition to operate greener vessels, with two further 'E-Flexer' vessels, the *Salamanca* and *Santoña*, to join sister-ship *Galicia* in 2022 and 2023.

Commitment to the French flag and French seafarers.

Support from farming cooperatives and shareholders, enriching regions, linking people, and facilitating trade.

The imperative of profitability, with on-going support from the regions, banks, and government.

One of the consequences of the Brexit vote was the increasing interest of Irish hauliers in avoiding delays and bureaucracy at UK ports that were inherent in the existing Landbridge arrangements by selecting intra-EU sailings operating directly from Ireland to France and Spain. This prompted an expansion of direct sailings and the arrival of several new entrants into the market. Brittany Ferries introduced its seasonal weekly Rosslare-Cherbourg sailing from 18th January 2021 with the *Cap Finistère*, later replaced by the regular vessel *Connemara*. Additional sailings brought the *Armorique* to operate a new weekly Roscoff-Cork midweek round trip from late March until May. However, the start of the seasonal passenger sailings from Ireland to France was deferred due to continued travel restrictions.

The temporary thrice-weekly crossings of the *Armorique* between Ireland and France introduced in February were reduced to two from early April, with the vessel utilised for a weekly Poole-St Malo crossing in place of one of the Irish sailings. The change brought an end to the arrangement where Rosslare was oddly served from St Malo with a weekly sailing inbound-only, and Cork having the opposite outbound-only link to St Malo. The new schedule saw the *Armorique* operating a weekly Roscoff-Cork-St Malo-Poole-St Malo-Cork-Roscoff rotation. Her sailings were reportedly very quiet and were suspended completely in early June when the *Armorique* was used to cover the Portsmouth-Le Havre route in place of the *Cotentin*, which was suffering technical problems. Her sailings did not resume and from mid-July she sailed between Portsmouth and St Malo. With travel restrictions continuing, the restoration of passenger services on the Cork-Roscoff, Rosslare-Bilbao and Rosslare-Cherbourg routes with the *Pont-Aven, Armorique*, and *Connemara*, which had been put back from 23rd March to 17th May, was further deferred, first until 6th June and then to 20th June.

As the pandemic waned through the early summer, the gradual re-opening of international travel from the UK was subjected to a government imposed, but opaque, 'traffic light' system. Spain was placed in a new 'amber' category, that required passengers to undertake a mandatory ten-day quarantine period when returning to the UK, making it impossible for many to consider taking a holiday. Spanish operations were handled by the *Galicia* until 6th June, when the *Pont-Aven* joined operations on the Plymouth-Santander link, operating twice-weekly. The Portsmouth-Bilbao service resumed on 28th June with the *Cap Finistère*. French services increased from mid-June despite France also being on the amber list; in a contrast to the UK stance, the French authorities determined that fully vaccinated UK travellers did not need to self-isolate on arrival. The Plymouth-Roscoff returned on 6th June with *Pont-Aven*, a full passenger service on the Portsmouth-Caen route commenced on 15th June with the *Normandie* and *Mont St Michel*, whilst the *Armorique* started the St Malo link on 27th June; the *Bretagne* returned to St Malo link on 13th September. But there were to be no summer passenger services from Poole.

On 5th August, fully vaccinated holidaymakers returning from France to the UK were no longer required to self-isolate; this allowed Brittany Ferries to gradually ramp up their operations over the next fortnight. The *Barfleur* retuned to open the Poole-Cherbourg service on 14th September, operating until the end of October, the *Bretagne* was due to re-enter service on the Portsmouth-St Malo link on 1st October for a period of one month prior to the *Pont-Aven* taking over the route for the remainder of the winter. The Portsmouth-Le Havre service remained closed until 2022.

Notwithstanding all the short-term revenue issues the Company continued to develop its 'green' credentials. Two further new hybrid LNG-electric E-Flexer ships were ordered by Stena RoRo for the Brittany Ferries fleet to replace the *Bretagne* and *Normandie*, with the vessels planned to enter service during 2024 and 2025. As well as

The *Normandie*, trend-setter of the nineties, will be withdrawn from the fleet in 2025 after 33 years service on the Portsmouth-Caen link. *(Darren Holdaway)*

significantly cutting emissions, these two new hybrid ferries will deliver lower levels of noise and vibration for passengers and improved passenger accommodation. The two new ships will be powered by cleaner LNG at sea and will be the first powered in this manner on the English Channel. They will also operate partially or completely on battery power, for example when arriving and departing port, and will plug in to shore-side power supplies for port operations when available from shore installations. This will allow recharging of onboard batteries and power for onboard systems like air conditioning, heating, and lighting, whilst cutting funnel emissions to zero whilst in port at the berth, thereby significantly improving port air quality. The vessels' large battery capacity will enable each to operate at speeds up to 17.5 knots using battery power alone.

The two 195-metre-long ferries (some 20m metres shorter than the *Galicia, Salamanca* and *Santoña*) are to be chartered from Stena RoRo on a ten-year agreement, with an option for Brittany Ferries to purchase them after four years. The entry into service of the new ship on the Portsmouth-Caen link will address the long-term imbalance in freight capacity created by the pitching of the *Normandie* against the *Mont St Michel*, which would have been addressed by the aborted new-build *Honfleur* in 2020.

The vessel will be bespoke designed to suit the Caen and St Malo routes on which they will operate, taking account of anticipated future trends for both passenger and freight traffic. A key element will be the longer and higher garage decks that will enable greater freight capacity and be better adapted to accommodate the trend towards larger cars that has been evident in the last 20 years. The present day Mini, for example, is 25 per cent longer and wider than the version that was on sale when the *Bretagne* was launched. The physical size of the garage allows the Company to address and accommodate the growing market for motorhomes. Meanwhile in-voyage charging will be available for electric car drivers, allowing them to fuel-up en route, ready for their arrival at destination.

The first ship in the new series will bring capacity of 2,377 lane metres, with 176 lane metres intended for passenger cars, and will have a passenger certificate for 1,400; meanwhile, the second ship will have 2,517 lane metres capacity, of which 1,388 lane metres will be intended for passenger cars.

Each ship will offer more cabins than the vessels they replace; there has been a long standing under provision of cabin accommodation on both routes, but especially on overnight crossings on the Portsmouth-St Malo route. Both new ferries will have an improved mix of cabin types, with a big increase in the number of high-end Commodore Class cabins. The *Normandie's* replacement will benefit from 30 more Commodore cabins, as well as a C-Club airport-style lounge. Meanwhile the *Bretagne's* replacement will have 79 more Commodore cabins, together with a C-Club lounge, as well as 18 more cabins for families of up to six people.

The arrival of these two vessels will bring the number of E-Flexer sisters operated by Brittany Ferries to five. There are substantial economies associated with the operation of a homogenous fleet, from staff and customer familiarity between vessels to engineering knowledge and the range of maintenance parts required; the company had not hitherto operated sister ships in the fleet until the delivery of the *Armorique* and *Cotentin*.

Christophe Mathieu observed that “Fleet renewal is not a choice for Brittany Ferries; it is an imperative to secure our future. Our customers rightly demand cleaner, greener, vessels and our port partners expect us to be good neighbours. Furthermore, we will certainly face tighter regulation in the years ahead. The future of our company depends upon our ability to rise to the challenge today to prepare for tomorrow. That is why I'm so proud to announce these new vessels.”

Freight relationships were enhanced when Brittany Ferries and French company CMA CGM entered a partnership to unlock synergies between the two companies in passenger and freight transport. CMA CGM agreed to invest €25 million in Brittany Ferries including €10 million in quasi-equity with a representative of the group joining the Brittany Ferries Supervisory Board. The partnership will enable CMA CGM to utilise freight space on Brittany Ferries services to expand the route structure and both companies expect to offer new freight services through the partnership. The two companies will work together on the rollout of LNG propulsion as an alternative to diesel fuel by sharing knowledge and resources in areas such as training for French crews and safety procedures.

The French government authorised a grant of €45 million to compensate for the passenger travel restrictions that saw Brittany Ferries' turnover fall by €220 million in 2020. The State also announced a €10 million waiver for debt and €6 million in aid from the Brittany region; President Macron also extended the payroll tax break for a further three years.

The *Cap Finistère*, acquired by Brittany Ferries in 2010, completed her final sailing from Spain on 30th October arriving at Portsmouth from Bilbao the following day. She then sailed for Cherbourg to discharge and crossed to Le Havre to be laid up alongside the *Pont-Aven* and *Bretagne*. Sold to GNV to become the *GNV Spirit*, she left Le Havre for Naples on 22nd February 2022.

Brittany Ferries took delivery of the *Salamanca* on 30thNovember 2021; the handover ceremony took place in Sweden at the head office of Stena RoRo. The *Salamanca* undertook sea trials in November in the yellow sea with a ship using LNG for the first time. Meanwhile a dedicated LNG simulator opened at the company's training centre in St Malo. Work also started on the provision of LNG bunkering terminals in Bilbao and Santander for the *Salamanca* and sistership *Santoña*; there were no plans for bunkering the vessels in Portsmouth or France.

The *Salamanca* undertook berthing trials at Bilbao, Santander, Brest, and Rosslare after her arrival in Europe from China. She was re-registered from the Cypriot to the French flag in Santander on 19th January 2022. On 5th February she was blessed in Roscoff and then sailed to Brest to take part in the 'One Ocean' summit. She drydocked at the Astilleros yard Santander in late February and left the shipyard on 7th March for Cherbourg. The *Salamanca* met the *Galicia* in Cherbourg for the first time on 14th March; the two vessels were joined by the *Bretagne* which sailed into the port form lay-up in Le Havre. The *Salamanca* entered service on 27th March between Bilbao, Portsmouth, and Cherbourg, operating two weekly services to Bilbao and

The *Cap Finistère* was sold to GNV to become the *GNV Spirit*; she seen here leaving Le Havre for Naples on 22nd February 2022. *(Pascal Bredel)*

Salamanca

Above: **Plaza Mayor Bar.** *(Brittany Ferries)*

Top right: **Azul Restaurant.** *(Brittany Ferries)*

Bottom right: **Club Lounge.** *(Brittany Ferries)*

Below: **Portside forward lounge.** *(Brittany Ferries)*

Fireworks accompany *Salamanca*'s first departure from Portsmouth on 27th March 2022. *(Brittany Ferries)*

one to Cherbourg to change crews.

The *Barfleur* covered for the absence of the *Normandie* until 26th March when she returned from refit in Poland. The *Bretagne* returned to the St Malo link after nearly 18 months laid up in Le Havre on 27th March. The following day the *Armorique* started operating from Roscoff to Plymouth, with a once-a-week operation to Cork. The Poole-Cherbourg link reopened on 29th March with the *Barfleur*; she had been laid up for nearly two years in Caen.

The second of the four LNG-fuelled E-Flexer ferries was floated out at the Jinling shipyard in China on 20th April 2022. The *Santoña* was built as a virtual sister to the *Salamanca* and the last of the first batch of vessels to be delivered by the Chinese shipyard. She was programmed to serve the Portsmouth-Santander route from 2023.

The first of the two LNG hybrid-fuelled vessels will be named *Saint-Malo* when she replaces the *Bretagne* from 2024; her 11.5 MWh electrical energy storage solution will be the largest in the world. New charging facilities will be provided at Portsmouth and St Malo during redevelopment works at each port.

Brittany Ferries new association with Condor enabled the resumption of fast craft services on the Portsmouth-Cherbourg and Poole-Cherbourg routes, using the sister company's *Condor Liberation*. The new seasonal service started on 27th May with sailings the week on Fridays, Saturdays, and Sundays. The link, operated and marketed by Brittany Ferries, ran until 4th September.

In a statement of commitment to Ireland-Spain services, the *Galicia* was earmarked to replace the *Connemara* on the Rosslare-Bilbao/Cherbourg roster from 2023. The new vessel expands both passenger and freight capacity on the routes. The twice weekly seasonal Roscoff-Cork crossings operated by the *Armorique* and *Pont-Aven* cease for the winter period

The *Honfleur* was completed by Fosen Shipyard after Brittany Ferries withdrew from the contract for her construction. In late 2022 she remains for sale by her new owners the Siem Group. *(Fosen Shipyard)*

at the end of October, returning in March 2023. The twice-weekly Rosslare-Bilbao sailings and weekly Cherbourg-Rosslare sailing continue with the *Connemara*, along with the weekend Le Havre-Rosslare round trip of the freighter *Cotentin*. The Visentini built *Connemara* was replaced during November 2022 by the *Salamanca* once that Portsmouth-Bilbao route closed for the winter, with the *Galicia* taking over permanently from March 2023 when the *Santoña* enters service on the Portsmouth-Santander route, freeing the vessel for the redeployment.

As Brittany Ferries began the celebrations to mark 50 years of operation, the Company can reflect on how the visionary intent of the founders had been successfully delivered over the ensuing decades. Although facing a daunting succession of challenges that repeatedly threatened the Company's existence, the resilience, commitment, and drive that characterised Alexis

SALAMANCA
SALAMANCA

Salamanca *(Darren Holdaway)*

Brittany Ferries' new E-Flexer *Salamanca* departs from Rosslare on 13th February 2022 following berthing trials at the port. Sister vessel *Galicia* started serving the port from November 2022. *(Gordon Hislip)*

An artist's impression of the *Saint-Malo* which is due to replace the *Bretagne* in 2024. *(Brittany Ferries)*

The *Santoña* is floated out. She will be a virtual sister to the *Salamanca* when she enters service on the Portsmouth-Santander route from 2023. *(Brittany Ferries)*

Gourvennec and his colleagues has enabled Brittany Ferries to overcome all the obstacles placed in its path and thrive. Creative partnerships forged with the French communities in which the Company is based have provided the long-term stability that competitors have lacked. With an ongoing fleet renewal programme destined to bring the benefits of homogenous vessels on a scale unmatched in the European ferry sector, Brittany Ferries can face the future with growing confidence.

Still owned by the original Breton agricultural co-operative shareholders, Brittany Ferries has grown to a pre-Covid-19 annual turnover of over €450 million and providing employment for up to 3,100 people at the peak, including 1,700 seafarers and 360 personnel in the UK. Services have expanded from the tentative Plymouth-Roscoff operation to embrace the ports of Portsmouth, Poole, Plymouth, Cork, Rosslare, Caen, Cherbourg, Le Havre, St Malo, Roscoff, Bilbao, and Santander, served by a fleet of twelve ships. Over 2.5 million passengers are carried in a 'normal' year, accompanied by almost 900,000 cars and 210,000 freight units.

Brittany Ferries retains its position as France's leading maritime transport operator, with an award-winning reputation for service, and continues to demonstrate its resilience in the face of challenging external events. A long-term perspective and a consistent investment in quality continues to serve Brittany Ferries well as the Company enters its second half century of operation.

What might have been: the Scottish Bretagne

by Matthew Murtland

BRITTANY FERRIES & GOVAN

In 1982 Brittany Ferries introduced the capable *Quiberon* on its Santander-Plymouth-Roscoff-Cork routes, adding capacity to this already successful operation. After just a few years however, even this larger ship was struggling to cope with the demand and with increasing passenger expectations. To this end, Brittany Ferries management, supported by a five-year plan produced for them by consultants Peat Marwick Mitchell, determined that a new, much larger, and purpose-built ship was needed, and tenders were invited from interested shipyards.

That vessel would eventually become the *Bretagne*, built at Chantiers de l'Atlantique (CDA) in Saint-Nazaire, but UK Government files recently declassified in the National Archives show how close this order came to being placed at the Govan yard of British Shipbuilders Ltd, on the Clyde.

THE GOVAN PROPOSAL

The Govan shipyard had a long and storied history, stretching back as far as 1834 and being best known as the Fairfield Shipbuilding & Engineering Co. In the late 1960s Fairfields became part of Upper Clyde Shipbuilders and later was nationalised and absorbed into British Shipbuilders in 1977.

In 1985, seeking to reverse years of decline in Clyde shipbuilding, the yard won the order for the *Norsea* for North Sea Ferries, the largest passenger ship built in the UK since the *Queen Elizabeth 2* in 1969. Significant amounts were spent on retraining workers and on new technology to fulfil the order with management confident that successful and timely delivery of this key reference ship would prove that Govan was a serious contender for similar orders for passenger ships from around the world, a market they felt was ripe for growth into the 1990s. However, no further ferry or cruise ship orders had been forthcoming by late 1986; whilst the yard was confident of soon winning a bid for some large Chinese container ships, there was still a looming gap in the order book into which the Brittany Ferries ship would nicely fill.

The ship that Govan proposed shared various basic elements with the *Bretagne* as she was when subsequently built in France. The side profile bears a resemblance to Jahre Line's *Kronprins Harald* of 1987 (later *Oscar Wilde*) and was clearly inspired by ferries of the 'large block principle' generation of the 1980s, with a general arrangement largely following the vertical split of cabins set forward and accommodation aft pioneered in its modern form by the *Finnjet* of 1977. In contrast the *Bretagne* as built would adopt a horizontal split which allowed for an appealing sweep of passenger saloons throughout Deck 7, with a full deck of cabins below.

The vehicle deck arrangements were similar to the *Bretagne*, with an upper car deck (Deck 5) above a full height freight deck with retractable mezzanine decks.

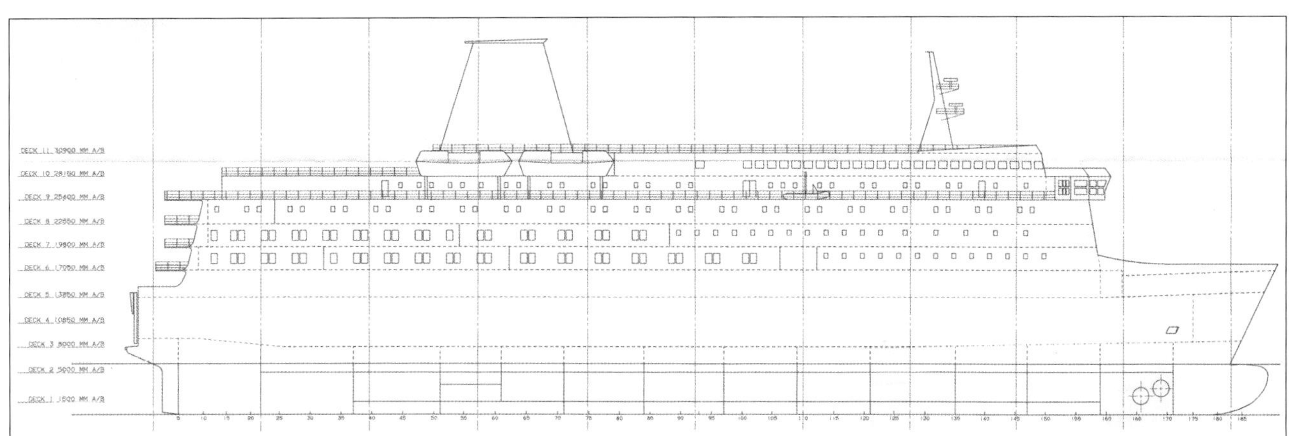

A simplified profile plan of the proposed Govan ship. Whilst some of the details such as the funnel arrangement would presumably have been finessed had the order been placed, in general the design appears more rectilinear and conservative than the *Bretagne*. *(Matthew Murtland collection)*

Bretagne *(FotoFlite)*

The vehicle decks were arranged around a central funnel casing offset to the port side, as on both *Norsea* and the *Bretagne*. The Govan vessel, however, left scope for the upper vehicle deck to be converted to drive-through loading, with the vents and bulkheads forward arranged in such a way that a central door could be added at some future point (in turn denying this design the area of passenger deck on the forecastle which is such a popular feature on the *Bretagne* as built.). The Govan proposal was also somewhat shorter, at approximately 142m in length, than the final ship's 151.2m and a total of 884 cabin berths were proposed (against 1,146).

The vertical arrangement grouped together the main bar/lounge, a Viennoisserie and the Duty Free shop together aft on Deck 6, the cafeteria and waiter service restaurant aft on Deck 7, and a small wine bar at the stern on Deck 8. Short arcades along the starboard sides of Decks 6 and 7 linked cabin areas to the public rooms but would have been narrower and less central to the design than the solution settled on in the *Bretagne*. The planned single-height main entrance lobby appears to be notably less spacious than that of the final vessel whilst the staircases between decks followed the *Norsea* in being compact and steep. The Govan proposal also included a top deck (Deck 10) 'sky lounge' full of reclining seats, similar to the *Duc de Normandie*, whereas the actual *Bretagne* had her seating areas lower down on Deck 8. Beneath the vehicle deck, on Deck 2, forward would be found a large, single cinema with tiered seating for 130 with additional passenger cabins just aft.

To meet Brittany Ferries' requirements Govan proposed a series of complicated financing arrangements by which shipbuilding subsidies and tax arrangements in the UK would be maximised, as well as registration subsidies and tax schemes in France for French owners and operators (part of this required the DTI to determine that the ship would not be

The building of the *Bretagne* with her funnel in the foreground. *(Matthew Murtland collection)*

considered an export for tax purposes). In its final version this suggested that the Brittany Ferries ship owning company SABEMEN could set up a UK subsidiary to buy the ship (meaning it would be UK-owned for British tax purposes) but could also be treated as (indirectly) French-owned for French accounting and flagging.

THE BID COLLAPSES

The competition for the order in December 1986 narrowed down to between Van der Giessen de Noord and Govan and, in early January, Govan were informed by Christian Michielini that they were the preferred bidder with their proposal meeting the operator's technical and commercial requirements.

It was at this stage that a French yard, Chantiers de l'Atlantique, made a last-minute appearance on the scene. CDA had recently unexpectedly lost the contract

The British-registered *Norsea* swings in King George Dock, Hull on her evening sailing to Rotterdam. *(Miles Cowsill)*

to build a pair of new Sitmar cruise ships and now had a gap in its building schedule (Sitmar had ordered their previous new ships at Saint-Nazaire but the latest pair, one of which survives as Ambassador Cruise Line's *Ambience*, went to Fincantieri in Monfalcone, Italy).

At a meeting in mid-January with UK government officials, management of British Shipbuilders expressed the view that Michielini wanted to build the ship at Govan, "but was coming under severe [political] pressure to have the vessel built at Saint-Nazaire". In an effort to get on the front foot the British Secretary of State for Trade and Industry Paul Channon took the unusual step of writing to his French counterpart, Alain Madelin, setting out the position, advising that "I understand no French shipbuilder can match the Govan offer without breaking [EEC regulations on subsidies for shipbuilding]… the competition from Govan is fair and it is vital that Britanny Ferries (sic) should place the order there soon. I can well understand your difficulties in this matter, but I believe that Chantiers d'Atlantique has work well into 1988 and therefore faces a far less serious situation than Govan".

Consistently mis-spelling 'Brittany Ferries' in his letter may not have helped Channon's cause (M. Madelin would never reply to this letter, something the British would later describe as "discourteous") but Madelin was in any event unlikely to be sympathetic to Govan's plight, having for many years represented a constituency in Ille-et-Vilaine, Brittany. He therefore had regional as well as national interests to defend and, with Brittany Ferries still dependent on regional funding, there were mechanics in place to exert political pressure. In response, one option the UK government considered, according to an internal memo, was "to put pressure on Brittany Ferries by the threat of instigating a full investigation into their operating subsidies. We have begun to play this card…"

Despite the rumours in the background, Christian Michielini and a large team came to London on 5th February to hammer out the details of the contract with British Shipbuilders. A memo prepared for the Secretary of State reported that Michielini appeared to be negotiating in good faith and had told them that Alexis Gourvennec had been to Paris to tell the government "to stop trying to block the order with Govan… that Brittany Ferries were already a year behind their chosen expansion and needed their new ship by May 1989 to take advantage of the summer season."

Michielini, the report continued, "said pressure appeared to have been eased on the political members of the Boards of Brittany Ferries… but there were still methods by which the French authorities could frustrate the deal. We are aware, for instance, that French registration for the vessel could be refused, which is essential for Brittany Ferries because of the public element in its ownership".

The issue hit the French press for the first time on 14th February with *Le Monde* carrying an article suggesting that Govan still had the more favourable bid and that they may get the Brittany Ferries order, with CDA being compensated with a new ship being planned for the state-owned Corsican operator SNCM. CDA, however, were clear that they could build both vessels and were being strongly supported to this end from the central government in Paris.

In a briefing note the Department of Trade & Industry (DTI) summed up the position: "Govan desperately needs the work. The *Norsea* for P&O is on target for delivery at the end of March and the other main prospect, container ships for China, is uncertain though final negotiations in Hong Kong at present seem to be going well, if very slowly. The prospect of a short-term conversion job remains difficult to assess. Beyond that, Govan is in the running for the St Helena ship [which became the Aberdeen-built RMS *St Helena* of 1990] but an order is not expected before the Summer."

The British therefore took the matter to the European Commission, requesting that they compare the bids, a move which provoked an angry response from French officials. A memo from Sir John Fretwell, the UK's Ambassador to France, stated that "the French claim to be shocked… In the past there had been a sort of tacit agreement amongst community countries not to poach national business from one another, which we were now breaching. [They] claimed that the [French] Ministry of Industry had in the past discouraged French yards from going all out to get orders in Britain and said that British shipowners had on several occasions made clear to the French that their

Les Abers Restaurant on the *Bretagne*. *(Miles Cowsill)*

Above: **The *Bretagne* leaves the port of St Malo on her nine-hour passage to Portsmouth.** *(Darren Holdaway)*

Left top: **Looking forward on the *Bretagne*.** *(Darren Holdaway)*

Left bottom: **Outside deck view from the bridge.** *(Darren Holdaway)*

Below: **A bridge view as the *Bretagne* leaves St Malo passing the Phare de Grand Jardin lighthouse.** *(Darren Holdaway)*

Top: The Café on Deck 8. *(Darren Holdaway)*

Middle: Le Yacht Club, Deck 7. *(Darren Holdaway)*

Above: The La Baule self service restaurant on Deck 7. *(Darren Holdaway)*

orders would stay in Britain."

In early April Govan successfully won the contract for the planned series of Chinese-owned container ships which relieved some of the pressure on the yard's future. The plans to become a serious player in the passenger ship market, however, hung on the French order and, as late as early May, Christian Michielini was still in contact with management suggesting the ship may yet be built there – but by this time Govan no longer felt able to meet the May 1989 delivery deadline.

Finally, on 7th May 1987, came confirmation that the decision had been made to place the order with the Saint-Nazaire yard. The following day French Prime Minister Jacques Chirac visited the Loire Atlantique region to announce that the arrangements for the order going to CDA were now in place, confirming it was supported by part of "several hundreds of millions of Francs" in subsidies for the French shipbuilding industry.

The final Govan bid was reported as the equivalent of FFR415m (£41m); CDA, whose earlier bid had been approximately FFR480m, had been able to reduce their offer to between FFR435m and FFR450m; British officials believed the cost to build the ship would actually be more than double this amount. When Brittany Ferries contacted Govan to confirm the news, they told them that, "other aspects of the bid… the political pressure and the structure of their shareholding" meant they had "no alternative but to accept the higher price".

In an interview with *The Scotsman* Govan's Managing Director, Eric Mackie, placed no blame on Brittany Ferries who had been placed in an impossible position. He explained that "we had the best bid, spent a lot of money and put a lot of design work and effort into that order… I won't be putting any more French mustard on my steaks."

LEGACY

Chantiers d'Atlantique delivered the *Bretagne* in July 1989, two months later than the May deadline Govan had been working to. CDA would go on to become one of the world's premier builders of cruise ships and is today, after the collapse of parent STX Europe, owned by the French government. As expected ,the yard was also given the contract for the new SNCM ship which had been intimated during the negotiations – in fact the *Danielle Casanova* and *Bretagne* ended up being built in parallel with both being delivered in the Spring/early Summer of 1989.

At Govan, despite the gap in activity after completion of the *Norsea* the two container ships for Chinese owners were eventually delivered in 1989 and 1990. By that point the yard had been denationalised and sold to Norwegian owners, becoming Kvaerner Govan. It is now part of BAE Systems and is engaged primarily in naval shipbuilding. Despite the high hopes of the late 1980s, no further passenger ships were constructed at Govan after the *Norsea,* and the latter remains the last large ship of her type to be built in the UK.

The *Bretagne,* of course, sails on into her fourth decade; we can only wonder what might have been for both ship and shipyard had Govan been allowed to win the order for her construction back in 1987.

A Channel Islands adventure

Brittany Ferries' involvement in Channel Island services came about almost by accident. When port facilities for the Caen service were completed by Portsmouth City Council, Brittany Ferries was not ready to open the new route but committed to pay additional port dues. The States of Jersey's desire to introduce competition on mainland shipping services prompted thoughts of a solution; if Brittany Ferries were part of a Channel Islands consortium, then port charges could be absorbed by the new venture.

Initial plans to use the *Penn-Ar-Bed* were thwarted, but a joint venture with Huelin Renouf and haulier Mainland Market Deliveries (MMD) established Channel Island Ferries and announced their new service on 8th August 1984. Services would operate on a year-round basis, overnight from Jersey and Guernsey with a daytime return crossing from Portsmouth. The *Bénodet,* renamed the *Corbière* after the iconic lighthouse in Jersey, was chartered to the venture, and Brittany Ferries provided systems and management support.

The *Corbière's* low-cost service was inaugurated from St Helier on 27th March 1985 and soon offered a popular contrast to privatised Sealink British Ferries' 'Bateau de Luxe' offering. By the end of August, Channel Island Ferries had carried 68,000 passengers, attracting 83% of the Portsmouth-Jersey market to force Sealink British Ferries to restructure their operation for 1986 after incurring a substantial loss. 1986 proved to be a difficult year with intense air competition biting into the sea market. There was only sufficient business to sustain one operator.

Talks between Channel Island Ferries and Sealink British Ferries considered consolidation of services, and

The *Corbière* inaugurated the new Channel Islands service from St Helier on 27th March 1985. The former Brittany Ferries vessel is seen here following the rebranding of the operation to British Channel Island Ferries. *(FotoFlite)*

The ***Corbière*** **dressed overall on her first arrival in St Helier on 23rd March 1985.** *(Dave Hocquard)*

In need of a repaint, the *Breizh-Izel* arrives in Portsmouth with a well-loaded BCIF freight sailing from the Channel Islands. (Miles Cowsill)

The *Armorique* operating for BCIF to cover for the stricken Rozel. *(Robert Le Maistre)*

eventually agreed a merger. The new joint venture was announced on 30th September 1986 when British Channel Island Ferries (BCIF) was launched. But Sealink British Ferries was unable to secure the cooperation of seafarers, who faced job losses and a radical change in working practices, and after a period of strike action with vessels blocking berths in Portsmouth, Weymouth, and Guernsey, was forced out of the venture. Channel Island Ferries remained the parent holding company for BCIF. Meanwhile, fast craft operator Condor took advantage of the limited capacity now available and deployed the passenger-only hydrofoil *Condor 7* from Weymouth.

The collapse of the joint venture left the *Corbière* operating alone on the service. The *Breizh-Izel* was chartered from Brittany Ferries to offer additional freight capacity, and a seasonal service from Weymouth began on 18th April 1987 with the former P&O Ferries *Lion*, renamed the *Portelet*. The *Cornouailles* was chartered from Brittany Ferries to sail in tandem with the *Portelet* and offer additional capacity for the Easter period. The *Corbière* and *Portelet* offered combined daily peak capacity for 2,190 passengers, substantially below the 3,800 offered by both operators in summer 1986.

Meanwhile, invigorated by the success of their short notice autumn 1986 operation, Condor signed an agreement to operate a seasonal summer service from Weymouth to the Guernsey and Jersey between 10th April and 17th October 1987, using the hydrofoils *Condor 5* and *Condor 7*. The service started from St Malo and ran via Jersey and Guernsey to and from Weymouth. Condor carried 46,200 passengers in their

From top in a clockwise direction: **The *Rozel* at St Helier, the Corbière Bar on the *Rozel*, the *Portelet* arriving in St Peter Port, the *Havelet* arriving in Guernsey from Poole, and the Steamship Restaurant on the *Rozel*.** *(All photos Miles Cowsill)*

British Channel Island Ferries intoduced the ***Rozel,*** the largest ever ferry on the Channel Island services, in 1989. She is seen here arriving at Poole to take up service on the link, with the ***Corbière*** having just completed her last sailing with the company. *(FotoFlite)*

The ***Reine Mathilde***, renamed the ***Beauport***, was another Brittany Ferries vessel deployed on BCIF service, seen here in St Peter Port, Guernsey. *(Miles Cowsill)*

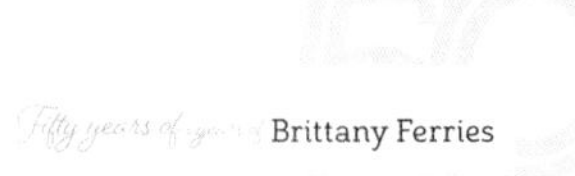

first full season of operation on the UK route.

Brittany Ferries' initial objective of offsetting port charges at Portsmouth through operation of the Channel Islands service had been fulfilled, and BCIF was adding to port congestion. BCIF services were transferred to Poole from 2nd January 1989, reducing the passage time by up to two hours and narrowing the journey differential with the Condor service from Weymouth. This was an unpopular move with the freight community and MMD and Commodore formed a joint venture to offer a replacement freight service from Portsmouth.

Reduction to a one-ship operation was achieved by chartering the 8,987-tonne *Scirocco* from Cenargo to replace the *Corbière* for the 1989 season. As the renamed *Rozel*, she brought capacity for 1,300 passengers and 296 cars, cabin accommodation for 671 passengers, and seating for a further 982. The *Corbière* was returned to Brittany Ferries for the Poole-Cherbourg service, and the *Portelet* was returned to Marlines on completion of her Weymouth season. In December Channel Island Ferries purchased the *Cornouailles* from Brittany Ferries, and she was renamed the *Havelet* after a £2 million refit at Brest.

On 26th September 1989, the *Rozel* struck rocks in St Peter Port harbour when arriving from Jersey and headed to Falmouth for repair, including a new propeller boss and rudder stock. The *Armorique* was brought from lay-up and took up the service on 28th September, before replaced by a loan of the *Reine Mathilde* from 9th October, with the *Armorique* returning to offer further assistance.

The switch to Poole initially proved successful, with a 20% rise in carryings to 499,022 passengers in 1989. Condor was also growing, and carried 85,191 passengers, giving the fledgling operation a significant 17% market share. BCIF marketed a 'French Connection' service in conjunction with Brittany Ferries and Emeraude Ferries to offer a Poole-Jersey, Jersey-St. Malo, St. Malo-Portsmouth round trip for the 1990 season.

The 1991 season was impacted by the Gulf War and Condor took a significant proportion of the sea business. Channel Island Ferries tried to purchase the *Rozel* but the Cenargo asking price was unrealistic, so the smaller *Reine Mathilde* was chartered for two years from Marine Invest, who had purchased her from Brittany Ferries. The vessel would be renamed the *Beauport*. With the conflicts of interest from their relationship with Commodore proving incompatible with a shareholding in Channel Island Ferries, MMD sold their shares and Brittany Ferries' interest was increased to 49%.

The *Rozel* made her last sailings to the Channel Islands in January 1992 and the *Beauport* entered service in February after a £1 million refit. On 24th August 1992 Condor announced plans to introduce two car-carrying wave-piercing catamarans to compete directly with BCIF from spring 1993. and TNT Shipping and Development took a 50% financial stake in Condor. At the end of the season and facing another downturn in carryings, BCIF announced a reduction in services for the 1993 season.

Condor's search for a second vessel for cross-channel operation proved difficult, and only the *Condor 10* operated in 1993. BCIF re-introduced the *Havelet* as a passenger vessel from 27th May to offer a twice-daily seasonal passenger service from Poole alongside the *Beauport*. An intense price war between BCIF and Condor escalated through the summer season, forcing rates downwards. By the end of the season BCIF was facing a £3 million loss and competition from Condor extending through the winter months. The charter of the *Beauport* was not renewed, and the company planned to operate passenger services with only the *Havelet* in 1994, supplemented by the *Purbeck*, which had been purchased by Channel Island Ferries from Brittany Ferries following arrival of the *Barfleur*. The *Beauport* undertook her final sailing for BCIF on 31st October and the *Purbeck* commenced duties the following day.

As before, there was insufficient business to sustain competitive operations. Talks between the parties resulted in BCIF ceasing passenger and freight services from 22nd January 1994 with Condor purchasing the passenger business, and Commodore buying the freight operation. All BCIF shareholders were reimbursed in full. Condor assumed a short-term charter of the *Havelet*, and Commodore took a longer-term charter of the *Purbeck*.

All mainland passenger sailings were transferred to Weymouth and freight sailings were concentrated in Portsmouth. The *Havelet* made her last sailing under BCIF management from Poole on 20th January, leaving the Channel Islands without any passenger service until 7th February, when the *Condor 10* returned to service. The *Havelet* made her final sailing for Condor under the charter arrangement on 29th October 1996 and was then laid up in Weymouth. The *Purbeck* charter was completed in 1995 and the vessel returned to management company Channel Island Ferries. The still active management company employed her on a succession of charters to Sally Line, Irish Ferries, Truckline, Gaelic Ferries, Falcon Seafreight, Brittany Ferries (for the Portsmouth-Caen service), Commodore Shipping and Tranz Rail in New Zealand. She was eventually sold to Toll NZ Consolidated Ltd on 8th March 2006.

Brittany Ferries returned to the Channel Islands as a minority partner in a joint venture with the Columbia Threadneedle European Sustainable Infrastructure Fund, which purchased the Condor business in March 2020.

Ship liveries and design of Brittany Ferries

When the *Kerisnel* debuted for Brittany Ferries in 1973 she was outfitted in a plain white colour scheme with the corporate initials 'BAI' painted on her twin funnels in black, with accompanying thin bands along the length of her hull. There was no attempt to incorporate the Company name on the hull, although this was becoming more commonplace elsewhere, notably in the bright orange and white hulls of Thoresen Car Ferries.

As the Company grew, so more attention was given to corporate identity. By the time the *Cornouailles* was delivered in 1977, a solid and chunky logo in Franklin Gothic condensed type was being widely applied across printed material and advertising. This was a representation of the interplay between the coastlines of Brittany and Southwest England in the earthy orange colour of vegetables. The logo was adopted on the ship's funnels, encapsulated in a wide navy-blue band; its blandness led to it being dubbed the 'Polish Railways' logotype. The hull remained white, with navy-blue and orange horizontal stripes representing the sea and the land, with the navy-blue stripe peaking at the bow.

The *Armorique* retained the funnel logotype on her arrival in 1976, but now the Company name was spelt out in lower case navy lettering along each hull, sandwiched in between the corporate motif depicted in orange on each side of the words 'brittany ferries', with the navy-blue and orange wraparound stripes reduced in thickness.

The Rook Dunning design studio created an updated look for Brittany Ferries in 1984. Their work employed a new Egyptian face with a slab serif introduced solidity and a sense of tradition, even though this was an unusual font to employ at this time. The new logo was designed to be a strong visual device that worked in

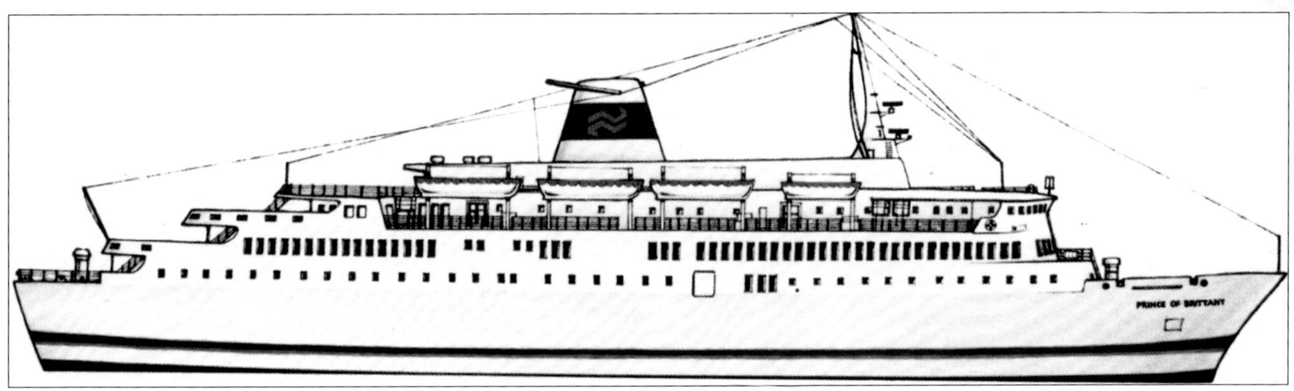

Top: The ***Prince of Brittany*** in her early days without Brittany Ferries wording to the hull. *(Ferry Publications Library)*

Middle: The ***Goelo*** showing her hull design incorporating the logo and Company name. *(Ferry Publications Library)*

Above: The ***Bretagne*** in her modifed livery of 1984 created by Rook Dunning Design. *(Ferry Publications Library)*

Below left: **New style uniforms were introduced for staff on entry into service of the *Normandie*.** *(Ferry Publications Library)*

Below right: **One of the strong branding images for Company brochures for many years was the funnel of the *Normandie*.** *(Ferry Publications Library)*

Left: **Funnel view of the *Pont l'Abbe.*** *(Miles Cowsill)*

Above: ***Mont St Michel.*** *(Miles Cowsill)*

multiple environments, from an A4 letterhead to the hull of each vessel. The practical considerations of how the device might be applied by a painter hanging from a crane trying to write letters twelve feet high on the side of a ship, were also taken into account. The ship proposal adopted a two tone 'wave' logo above the name, now with each word capitalised, with the new strapline 'The Holiday Fleet' used in advertising. The new corporate identity retained the earth and sea stripe along each vessel's white hull, which was reflected in the colours of the new logo. It was a case of gradualism rather than revolution. There was no desire to undertake a rapid roll-out of the new livery, so it was applied the next time each vessel was due to be repainted. However, the use of stencils resulted in the funnel logo being applied back-to-front on several vessels, but this discrepancy went unremarked. Several iterations of orange and red colours were applied before a final colour evolved.

A further development of Brittany Ferries' corporate identity was commissioned in 2004 in an adaptation of the previous scheme, representing further evolution of the design. The corporate name received a softer italicised sans serif font, with the wave motif extended in length on both the ships' hulls and funnels. The navy-blue and orange stripes were shortened in length to leave the bow and stern sections in plain white.

This variation of the livery was to endure but changing tastes and the Company's further growth and expansion prompted extensive customer research to understand perceptions of the brand. Introducing a new identity in 2019, Florence Gourdon, marketing

director explained that "We last evolved our logo 15 years and so much has changed in that time – for example we now live in a digital world. And while the previous logo fully communicated the reliability and trustworthiness of our ferry service, it didn't fully embody the emotional side of travelling and holidaying with Brittany Ferries and the discoveries inherent in the fabulous destinations we serve."

The new design was said to reflect the fullness of the ferry operator's experience: the richness of travel by sea, the warmth of the welcome ashore and on board, and the spirit of discovery for some of Western Europe's most beautiful holiday destinations. A new colour was added to the palette, with green added to the traditional corporate navy-blue and orange. The new logotype incorporated a more modern, warm, and lyrical typeface, with blue, green, and orange shades evoking the seas, landscapes and skies of the holiday regions served by Brittany Ferries. The hull motif was repositioned from above to ahead of the corporate name.

Gourdon added "This new look stands for everything that makes our brand: the quality of our products and services, the passion, pride and professionalism of our teams, and our bright future with brand new ships and rich experiences on the horizon."

The new design was gradually rolled out across the fleet. As with previous iterations it was also incorporated in Brittany Ferries marketing and operations including everything from signs, brochures, uniforms, to advertising and websites. Consistent with Brittany Ferries' business approach the corporate identity journey has been characterised by progressive evolution, with each iteration of the design building on the last, and still paying subtle homage to the Company's roots.

The *Pont Aven* showing the pre-2019 livery. *(Miles Cowsill)*

Brittany Ferries

— France & Spain —

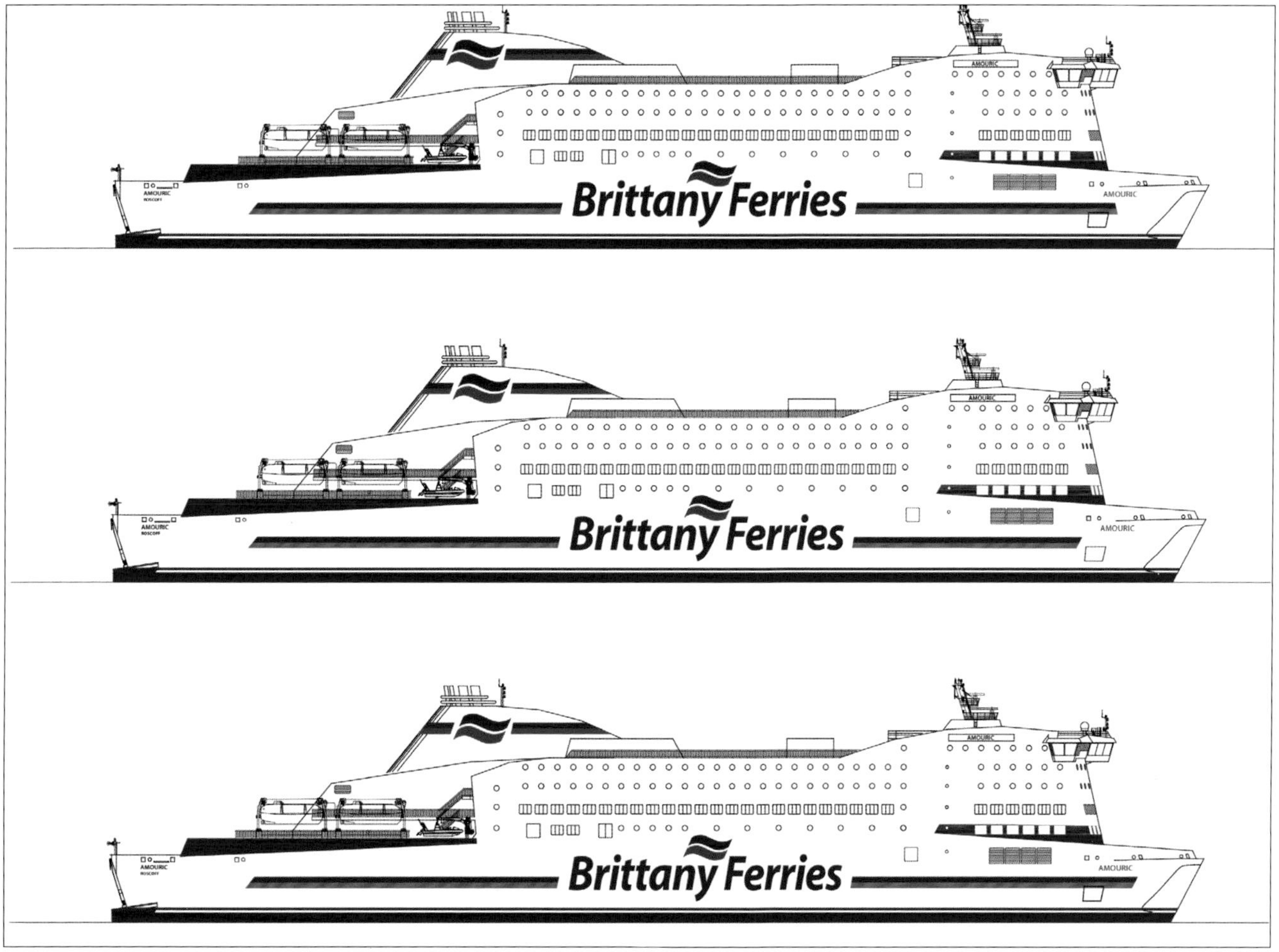

Brittany Ferries

AMOURIC

Brittany Ferries

AMOURIC

Brittany Ferries

AMOURIC

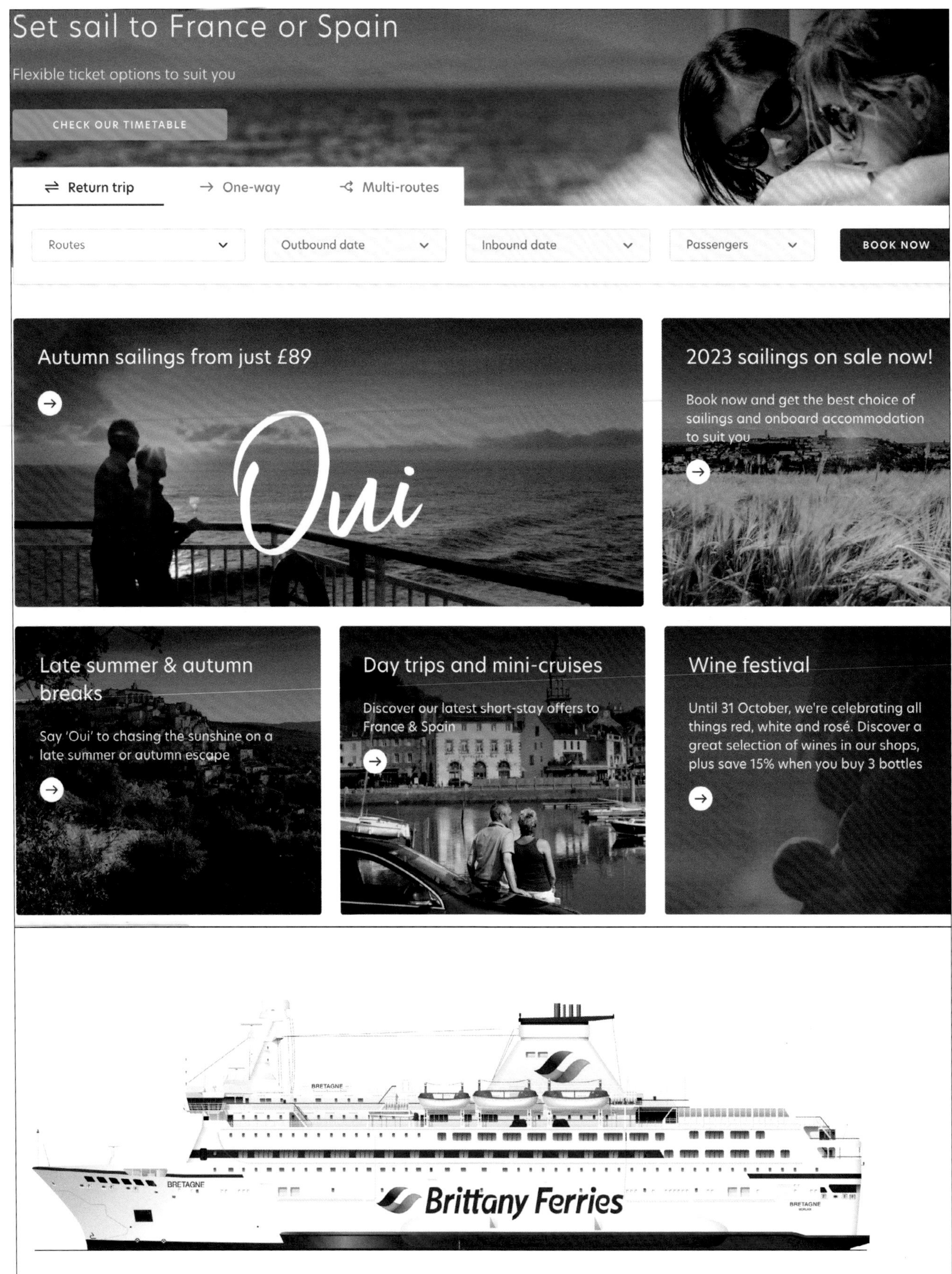

Top: **In 2022 Brittany Ferries runs an efficent and easy to follow web site; long gone are the days of brochures and call centres to promote and market the business.** *(Brittany Ferries)*

Above: **The *Bretagne* in the new corporate livery of 2019.**

The new logo and branding of Brittany Ferries introduced in 2019 is portrayed here on the ***Cotentin*** and ***Armorique***. *(Pascal Bredel)*

MONT ST MICHEL
CAEN
SCANIA
SCANIA
OPEX

Mont St Michel **and *Salamanca*** *(Mike Louagie)*

Fleet List 1973-2022

	Built	Gross tons	Length	Passengers	Cars	Freight	Brittany Ferries service
Ailsa Princess	1971	3,715	116	1,800	190	-	1982
Armorique	1972	5,732	117	700	170	-	1976-1993
Armorique (2)	2009	29,468	167	1,500	470	65	2009-
Baie de Seine	2003	22,382	199.4	596	316	154	2015-2020
Barfleur	1992	20,133	158	1,212	550	112	1992-
Beaverdale	1977	5,669	116	12	-	65	1987, 1989
Bénodet	1970	4,238	108	1,200	260	26	1983-1984
Bonanza	1972	2,718	95	750	200	-	1976
Breizh-Izel	1970	2,769	112	12	-	65	1980-1987
Bretagne	1989	24,534	151	2,056	580	84	1989-
Cap Finistère	2001	32,828	204	1,608	1,000	140	2009-2021
Celtic Pride	1972	7,801	127	1,000	170	20	1987-1988
Condor Vitesse	1997	5,007	87	800	200	-	2001-2007
Connemara	2007	26,500	187	800	170	140	2018-
Cornouailles	1977	3,383	110	550	205	40	1977-1989
Cotentin	2007	22,308	168	213	-	120	2007-
Coutances	1978	2,736	110	58	-	800	1986-2007
Dania	1972	722	105.3	12	-	480	1979
Duc de Normandie	1978	13,505	131	1,500	320	528	1986-2005
Duchesse Anne	1979	9,796	122	1,500	332	39	1989-1996
Étretat	2008	26,500	187	800	185	120	2014-
Falster (Prince de Bretagne)	1975	2,424	118	346	250	-	1975
Faraday	1980	2,932		12	-	1,230	1980
Gabrielle Wehr	1978	1,599	108	12	-	1,148	1988-1989
Galicia	2021	42,000	215	1,000	300	180	2021-
Goelo	1967	5,073	111	1,170	210	- 1	980-1982
Gotland	1973	6,642	124	1,670	300	-	1988
Kerisnel	1972	3,395	99	12	-	540	1972-1974

The *Barfleur* seen as the *Deal Seaways* during her brief spell on charter to DFDS on their Dover-Calais service. *(FotoFlite)*

The early morning sun catches the *Pont Aven* as she arrives at Santander on her 23-hour passage from Plymouth. *(Miles Cowsill)*

	Built	Gross tons	Length	Passengers	Cars	Freight	Brittany Ferries service
Kerry	2001	24,418	186	1,000	75	156	2019-2020
Miseva	1972	6,057	118	12	-	552	1987
MN Pelican	1999	12,076	155	12	-	115	2016-
Mont St Michel	2002	35,592	173	2,120	874	2,250	2002-
Munster	1968	4,067	110	1,000	220	-	1979
New build	2025	30,000	194	1,310	470	120	2025-
Normandia	1970	2,312	118	12	-	636	1979
Normandie	1992	27,541	161	2,160	648	126T	1992-
Normandie Express	2000	6,581	97	900	260	-	2005
Normandie Shipper	1973	4,078	142	36	-	1,050	1989-1999
Normandie Vitesse	1997	5,005	87	741	200	-	2001-2012
Olau West	1963	3,061	97	1,500	180	-	1976
Penn-Ar-Bed	1974	2,891	104	250	235	-	1974-1984
Pont l'Abbe	1978	19,589	153	1,120	375	45	2006-2009
Pont-Aven	2004	41,589	184	2,400	650	85	2004-
Poseidon	1964	1,358	67	805	-	-	1973
Prince de Bretagne	1075	2,424	110	346	250	46	1975
Prince of Brittany (Reine Mathilde)	1970	5,464	120	1,020	210	20	1978-1988 1989-1991
Purbeck	1978	6,507	110	58	-	60	1986-1994, 1997, 2000-2002
Quiberon	1975	7,927	129	1,140	252	540	1982-2002
Regina	1972	8,020	127	1,000	170	-	1979
Saint-Malo	2024	30,000	195	1,290	370	63	2024-
Salamanca	2022	42,000	215	1,000	300	180L	2022-
Santoña	2023	42,000	215	1,000	300	165L	2023-
Skarvøy	1974	3,710		12	-	695	1990
Stena Searider	1973	3,209	142	12	-	83	1986-1987
Trégastel	1971	3,998	118	1,500	370	25	1985-1991
Val de Loire	1987	31,360	162	2,280	570	1,250LM	1993-2006
Valérie	1972	3,390					1974
Viking 1	1970	4,485	109	1,200	260	26	1982

Old ships in new waters

The *Quiberon* was sold in 2002; she is seen here in Medmar colours running under her old French name. She later operated between Spain and Africa going to to the breakers in India in 2010. *(Frank Lose)*

The *Penn-Ar-Bed* was sold to Marlines of Greece and was scrapped at Alang in India in September 2004. *(Ferry Publications Library)*

The former *Cornouailles*, seen in 2007 as the ***Sveti Stefan*** operating between Bar and Bari (Italy). She was withdrawn from service in 2013 and sold to breakers in Turkey. *(Bruce Peter)*

After completing service with BCIF in 1989, the 20-year old vessel was sold for further service in Greece. She was renamed ***Duchess M*** for operations between Italy and Greece following an extensive rebuilding programme, operating until 2014. *(Ferry Publications Library)*

The former ***Val de Loire*** is currently employed on the Newcastle-IJmuiden route as the ***King Seaways.*** She is seen here arriving in IJmuiden following her overnight sailing from the UK. *(Frank Lose)*

The former ***Pont l'Abbe*** still remains in service for Moby Lines as the ***Moby Corse.*** *(Frank Lose)*

The smart looking ***GNV Spirit*** (ex ***Cap Finistère***) was sold by Brittany Ferries in 2022 to GNV for service between Barcelona and Palma de Mallorca. *(Frank Lose)*

Built in 1979 for B&I Line as the ***Connacht*** and sold to Brittany Ferries in 1988 as the ***Duchesse Anne;*** the former Irish Sea vessel still remains in service today as the ***Dubrovnik*** after operating between Croatia and Italy for 26 years. *(Darren Holdaway)*

After her charter to Brittany Ferries as the *Goelo*, the former Viking Line ship saw a further brief spell on the English Channel with Sally Line before joining Moby Lines. She remained in service as the *Moby Dream* for nine years before becoming the *Sardegna Bella* of Sardegna Lines. In 2001 she was withdrawn from service and sold for scrap. *(Ferry Publications Library)*

The *Beauport* had a very mixed career after she completed operations on the Channel Islands before being sold for scrapping in India in 2000. *(Ferry Publications Library)*

Brittany Ferries sold the ***Duc de Normandie*** in 2005. She is pictured here leaving the Spanish port of Almeria as the ***Wisteria*** still looking very much the same as her days with the Company. She remained in service in the Mediterranean until 2020 and was sold for scrap in Turkey the following year. *(Miles Cowsill)*

The former ***Armorique*** leaving Hong Kong for Xiamen as the ***Min Nan*** following sale in 1993. Fire broke out on board her in 2011 off Madura, East Java when the vessel was heading towards Makassar, South Sulawesi. The captain gave the order to abandon ship and she later sank. *(Ferry Publications Library)*

Acknowledgements

This book would not have been possible without the significant contributions from many individuals who gave generously of their time to Ferry Publications over the years and who have helped also research detail from their own and other archives of material.

The authors would like to thank the following: Matthew Murtland, Pascal Bredel, John Hendy, Darren Holdaway, Philippe Holthof, Brian D Smith, Frank Lose, Mike Louagie, Kevin Mitchell and Ian Carruthers.

We would like to thank all those in Brittany Ferries who have made us so welcome over the years from shore staff on both sides of the Channel to officers and crews.

The biggest thanks go to our wives Linda and Christina, who have patiently supported and encouraged this project throughout.

Pascal Bredel